# The Spinning Heart
## Comparative Study Guide

A SCENE BY SCENE GUIDE

Amy Farrell

SCENE BY SCENE
WICKLOW, IRELAND

Copyright © 2019 by Scene by Scene.

Without limiting the rights under copyright, this book is sold subject to the condition that it shall not, by way of trade or otherwise be lent, resold, hired out, reproduced, stored on or introduced into a retrieval system, or transmitted, in any form or by any means (electronic, mechanical, photocopying, recording or otherwise), or otherwise circulated, without the publisher's prior consent, in any form other than that in which it is published and without a similar condition, including this condition, being imposed on the subsequent publisher.

All rights reserved. No part of this publication may be recorded or transmitted in any form or by any means electronic, mechanical, photocopying, recording or otherwise without the proper consent of the publisher.

The publisher reserves the right to change, without notice, at any time, the specification of this product, whether by change of materials, colours, format, text revision or any other characteristic.

Scene by Scene
Wicklow, Ireland.
www.scenebyscene.ie

The Spinning Heart Comparative Study Guide by Amy Farrell.
ISBN 978-1-910949-75-7

Cover photo © Volodymyr Melnyk

# Contents

| | |
|---|---|
| Chapter 1 - Bobby | 2 |
| Chapter 2 - Josie | 15 |
| Chapter 3 - Lily | 21 |
| Chapter 4 - Vasya | 27 |
| Chapter 5 - Réaltín | 32 |
| Chapter 6 - Timmy | 37 |
| Chapter 7 - Brian | 44 |
| Chapter 8 - Trevor | 51 |
| Chapter 9 - Bridie | 57 |
| Chapter 10 - Jason | 63 |
| Chapter 11 - Hillary | 68 |
| Chapter 12 - Seanie | 73 |
| Chapter 13 - Kate | 79 |
| Chapter 14 - Lloyd | 83 |
| Chapter 15 - Rory | 88 |
| Chapter 16 - Millicent | 94 |
| Chapter 17 - Denis | 99 |
| Chapter 18 - Mags | 105 |
| Chapter 19 - Jim | 109 |
| Chapter 20 - Frank | 116 |
| Chapter 21 - Triona | 124 |
| Cultural Context/Social Setting | 135 |

| | |
|---|---:|
| Literary Genre | 140 |
| General Vision and Viewpoint | 151 |
| Theme/Issue - Relationships | 158 |
| Hero, Heroine, Villain | 162 |
| Selecting Key Moments | 166 |
| The Comparative Study: Comparing Texts | 168 |

## About This Book

This book is a companion guide for the Comparative Study of *The Spinning Heart*, by Donal Ryan. Ideally it accompanies a second, detailed reading and study of the novel.

Each chapter contains notes on Cultural Context/Social Setting, Literary Genre, General Vision and Viewpoint, Relationships and Hero/Heroine/Villain, and a set of questions on Cultural Context/Social Setting, Literary Genre, General Vision and Viewpoint, Relationships and Hero/Heroine/Villain. The notes are intended as a starting point for students, to provide something concrete for each mode that can be developed and built on by exploring the relevant mode-based questions.

Towards the back of the book, there are notes looking at each mode as a whole, across the entire novel, and accompanying questions (please note, there may be some similarity with earlier questions to draw attention to key ideas).

Lastly, there is a section of questions on each mode, designed to prompt comparisons between *The Spinning Heart* and other Comparative Study texts.

# Chapter 1
# Bobby

Bobby talks about his hatred of his father, how he lost his job and his wife Triona and how highly he thinks of her.

## Cultural Context/Social Setting

The novel is set during the economic recession, a time of financial collapse in Ireland. Bobby, a former foreman on building sites, is out of work and struggling financially.

This is a rural community, where everyone knows each other and one another's business.

Bobby finds it difficult to really talk and express himself emotionally to his wife, suggesting that men are not encouraged to act this way in this world.

1. Why did Bobby trust Pokey Burke?
   What does this tell you about the community?

2. What did Pokey Burke do to his workers?

3. Describe Bobby's financial situation.
   What made his turn of fortune so unexpected?

4. Why did none of the men care what sort of a man Pokey Burke was?
   What does this suggest about their priorities?

5. How did people react to the death of the Cunliffe boy?
What does this reveal to you about this community?

6. What stopped Bobby from showing that he was clever in school?

7. Speaking of the Burkes, Triona says, "The whole village knows what they've done."
What insight does her comment give you into the world of the novel?

8. According to Triona, what makes local people think highly of Bobby?
What does this tell you about their values and attitudes?

9. Speaking to Triona, Bobby says, "I laughed then, through my invisible tears."
Why are his tears invisible?
What insight does this give you into this world?

10. How did the drinkers of Ciss's front bar feel about Bobby's father?
What does this tell you about this world?

11. What was life like for Bobby and his mother, living with his father?
What does this tell you about this world?

12. What did Triona's friend say about Bobby's family when Bobby met Triona at the disco?
What do her comments reveal about this world and characters' attitudes?

13. "Imagine it being found out, that you went to see a play, on your own."
    What insight does this comment give you into the lives of men in this world?
    Fully explain your point of view.

14. What picture are you forming of this place?
    Include as many significant details as you can.

## Literary Genre

Bobby, the novel's protagonist, speaks directly to the reader in this chapter. He is open, honest and sincere, and his voice instantly forges a connection with the reader.

Bobby reveals his intense hatred for his father, and details how vicious and cruel the man is. He admits to thoughts of murdering him, which adds excitement and suspense to his account.

Bobby's stories and anecdotes add to the reader's sense of him as a real person, while also explaining why he feels as he does about his father. This is an emotionally charged, confessional account, where Bobby tells the reader things he cannot bring himself to speak to his wife about. This makes us want to read on, while developing our sense of Bobby as a sensitive, troubled, caring character.

1. Read the first page of the novel again.
   How does it capture your imagination and arouse your curiosity?

2. What does the image of a "flaking, creaking, spinning heart" add to the opening?

3. Bobby says his wife let herself down by marrying him. What does this tell you about how Bobby feels about himself?

4. Bobby mentions the Cunliffe boy. What seems to have happened here? Does Bobby give a complete version of events? What is the effect of this on the story?

5. How does Bobby's exchange with Josie Burke add to your understanding of his character?

6. Bobby describes different ways he could kill his father. Comment on the imagery here. What do these descriptions add to the story?

7. What does Bobby's account of his father drinking out the farm add to the novel?

8. Bobby's father stopped drinking once his inheritance was spent. What does this tell you about him?

9. What are your impressions of Triona? What does she bring to the story?

10. What are your impressions of Bobby's father (Frank)? What does he bring to the story?

11. What are your impressions of Bobby after reading this chapter? Use examples to support your view.

12. Does it feel like Bobby Mahon is speaking directly to you in this chapter?
    How is this achieved?
    What is the effect of this on the reader?

13. Is the tone of this chapter confessional?
    Explain your point of view.

14. Are you sympathetic towards Bobby?
    Fully explain your point of view.

## General Vision and Viewpoint

The outlook in this chapter is dark and troubled. Bobby hates his father. This damaged relationship, his father's bitterness and Bobby's thoughts of murder, create a dark, bleak outlook.

Pokey Burke's treatment of his workers reveals the worst in human nature, as he absconds, leaving them without any hope of welfare assistance, having not paid what he should have to Revenue.

Speaking of his mother's death, Bobby's loss and regret are clear. His father destroyed Bobby's bond with his mother, another saddening aspect to the chapter's outlook.

Bobby's father's determination in drinking out the farm reveals how bitter and spiteful he is. He is a destructive character, delighting in causing hurt, revealing the vicious side of human nature.

There is also a positive aspect to this chapter. Bobby loves his wife, Triona and thinks the world of her. His devotion and sincere feeling here shows all that is warm and loving in human nature and life.

1. Bobby visits his father daily, hoping to find him dead.
   What is your response to this?

2. "There wasn't a stamp paid in for any of us, nor a screed to the Revenue, either."
   What did Pokey Burke do to his workers?
   How does this make you feel?

3. Bobby feels his wife let herself down by marrying him.
   How does this make you feel?

4. Describe how Bobby feels about his wife, Triona.
   Does their relationship highlight a positive or negative side of life?

5. What impact has his relationship with Triona had on Bobby?
   Has she made his life better?

6. Bobby refers to the death of the Cunliffe boy.
   How do the details of this story affect the mood at this point?

7. How did Bobby feel about going to see Josie Burke?
   How does this make you feel?

8. How did Josie Burke treat Bobby when Bobby went to see him?
   How does this make you feel?
   Does this highlight the good or the bad in people?

9. Bobby finds it difficult to speak openly with his wife about what is troubling him.
   How does this make you feel?
   How does this affect the general vision and viewpoint?

10. Bobby considers the different ways he could kill his father.
    How does this affect the story's outlook?
    How does this make you feel?

11. Why was Bobby jealous of Seanie Shaper growing up?
    How does this affect the general vision and viewpoint?

12. How does the story of Bobby's father drinking out the farm add to the general vision and viewpoint?

13. How did the other drinkers feel about Bobby's father?
    Is this a positive or negative aspect to the portrayal of life here?

14. Did Bobby's father make friends with the other drinkers?
    How does this affect the outlook?

15. What made Bobby's father drink out the farm?
    Comment on his motivation.

16. What sort of life did Bobby and his mother have, living with Bobby's father?
    How does this make you feel?

17. Bobby describes himself as "an orphan child, bereft, filling up with fear like a boat filling with water."

How is Bobby feeling?
How does this affect the general vision and viewpoint?

18. Bobby's last topic of conversation is his wife, Triona. How does this section affect the general vision and viewpoint?

19. How do you feel, reading this chapter? What stands out for you as being particularly positive or negative?

20. Is there darkness in this chapter? Explain your point of view.

# Relationships

Bobby and his father have a very negative, destructive relationship. Bobby hates his father, eagerly hoping for his death. His father is aware of this, and seems to spitefully enjoy it.

Bobby spends a lot of time thinking about killing his father, such is his hatred of him.

Bobby's father 'drank out the farm', spending every penny of his inheritance on drink to spite his own dead father. This shows how bitterly he hated his father, and gives an insight into the dysfunctional, destructive nature of his relationships.

Bobby and his mother could never be relaxed or happy around his father, who found fault with everything. Their relationship was eroded and compromised by Bobby's father.

When his mother died, Bobby wished he could go back and do things differently. There is a great sense of sorrow, regret and longing here, as

Bobby reveals what he has lost, and how his father stole his bond with his mother from him. Bobby's family relationships have led to hurt, suffering and sadness.

Bobby thinks very highly of his wife, believing that he is not good enough for her. Bobby wishes he were able to express himself properly to Triona, instead of her having to guess what he is thinking. He is unable to find the words to tell her what she wants him to.

1. Read the opening paragraph of this chapter again.
   What does it reveal to you about Bobby's relationship with his father?
   Is this a positive or negative relationship?

2. What effect did Bobby losing his job have on his father?
   What does this suggest about how he feels about his son?

3. How does Bobby view his wife?
   How does she feel about him?
   Is this a negative or positive relationship?

4. According to Bobby, how was his mother affected by her marriage to Bobby's father?
   How does this make you feel?

5. How did Josie Burke treat Bobby when Bobby went to see him?

6. How does Triona react to the way Josie treats Bobby?
   What does this tell you about how she feels about Bobby?

COMPARATIVE STUDY GUIDE • 11

7. "I wish to God I could talk to her the way she wants me to, besides forever making her guess what I'm thinking." What insight does Bobby's comment give you into his marriage?

8. How does Bobby's father feel about him, in Bobby's opinion?

9. What made Bobby jealous of Seanie Shaper when he was growing up?
What does this tell you about Bobby's family?

10. What sort of relationship did Bobby's father have with his own father?
What does this add to your understanding of the relationships in this novel?

11. What will Bobby never forgive his father for?

12. What was it like for Bobby and his mother, living with his father?
How did he affect their lives?

13. What did Bobby want to do on the day his mother was buried?
What does this tell you about his relationship with his mother?
What does this tell you about how his father treated Bobby and his mother?

14. Do Bobby's parents sound like good parents?
Use examples to explain your point of view.

15. Why was Pokey Burke afraid of Bobby?
What does this tell you about Bobby's relationship with Pokey?
What does this tell you about Bobby's relationship with Triona?

16. How does Bobby feel about Triona?
How does Triona feel about him?
What strengths do you see in their relationship?
What weaknesses do you see in their relationship?
Overall, is it a positive or negative relationship?
Explain your point of view.

17. Describe Bobby's relationship with his father.
How does he view his father? Quote to support your view.

18. From reading this chapter, do characters appear to communicate well with one another?
How does this affect them?

19. Do relationships bring characters happiness or sorrow?
Use examples to explain your point of view.

## Hero, Heroine, Villain

Bobby hates his father, wishing he were dead. He has suffered because of his father's vicious, bitter ways, and has missed out on the chance to enjoy his bond with his mother. He resents his father for this.

Bobby seems insecure and has a low opinion of himself. He feels that Pokey Burke took him for a fool, and does not believe that he is good enough for his wife, Triona.

Bobby thinks very highly of Triona, feeling that he is a better person because of his relationship with her.

Bobby was scared to go and face Pokey Burke's father, Josie Burke. Josie Burke speaks down to him, and Bobby is disappointed in himself for taking this bad treatment.

1. How does Bobby feel about his father?

2. How does Bobby feel about his wife?

3. What stopped Bobby from showing that he was clever in school?
   What does this tell you about Bobby?

4. Why was Bobby disappointed in himself after talking to Josie Burke?

5. According to Triona, how do local people view Bobby?

6. What stops Bobby from telling his wife how he feels?
   How does his inability to be open with Triona make him feel about himself?

7. Bobby spends a lot of time thinking about killing his father.
   Is Bobby a dangerous man?
   Fully explain your point of view.

8. Does reading about Bobby's father drinking out the farm affect how you feel about Bobby?
   Explain your point of view.

9. How did Bobby feel about his mother?
   What damaged their relationship?

10. Is Bobby a 'good' man?
    Explain your point of view.

11. What stands out for you about Bobby in this chapter?
    Include examples in your answer.

# Chapter 2
# Josie

Josie regrets the way he treated Bobby and feels ashamed of himself. He is ashamed of what Pokey has done.

## Cultural Context/Social Setting

Josie describes a lifetime of work, showing it is important in this world.

He feels a deep sense of shame for what Pokey has done, filled with regret at the deceitful way that Pokey has treated honest men. This shows that there is a moral code in this world, even if Pokey does not abide by it.

Josie refers to confession and God at several points in this chapter, showing how much a part of his life, and culture, religion is.

1. How did Pokey get into financial trouble?

2. What does Josie's chapter suggest about the roles of men and women in this world?
   Use examples to support your ideas.

3. What reasons does Josie have for not wanting to talk to his daughter?
   What insight does this give you into this society, its values, and how women are treated and viewed?

4. Where did Josie work in the sixties?
   How did his boss treat him?

5. How did men react when Josie tried to force himself on a woman one time?
What does this tell you about this world?

6. "When I think about it, what people must be thinking and saying, I can hear my heart beat in my chest."
How does Josie feel about what Pokey has done?
What makes him feel this way?
What does this tell you about this world?

7. How does Josie describe the housing sector at the end of the chapter?
What insight does this give you into this world?

8. Is Josie religious?
Does he make a lot of religious references?
What does this tell you about this world?

## Literary Genre

Josie's tone is open, honest and confessional. He admits his failings, his lack of real feeling for Pokey and his daughter, and the shame he feels for the way Pokey treated his workers. This honest style echoes that of Bobby in the opening chapter, while adding another layer to the narrative.

Mentioning the Cunliffe boy's death and the selling of his land, Josie suggests that things would always end badly for those making money from unhappy circumstances. He creates a sense that disaster was fated and inescapable, an almost superstitious fatalism. In this way he echoes and reinforces the sense of loss and regret from Bobby's account, further adding to the mood.

The Cunliffe boy's story remains a mystery, further engaging with the reader's curiosity.

1. How does Josie view Bobby Mahon?
   Quote to support your view.

2. How does Josie feel about what Pokey did to his workers?
   What does this add to the story?

3. What does the reference to the Cunliffe boy add to this chapter?
   Fully explain your point of view.

4. Is Josie honest in his account?
   Find examples to support your view.

## General Vision and Viewpoint

Josie is filled with regret; he regrets how he spoke to Bobby Mahon, how he was fixated with work, how he treated his wife. This sense of regret and wishing to change the past adds sadness to the outlook.

The shame he feels at Pokey's treatment of his workers further saddens the tone, adding to the sense of loss Bobby created in the first chapter.

As the chapter ends, there is the sense of a shadow hanging over the community. Josie says how the housing boom began for them with tears when the Cunliffe boy got shot and his land was parcelled out. He suggests that this was no way for good times to start, creating a sense of foreboding and negativity. In Josie's eyes, the good times, the thriving building trade, could never last given how it began, a dark and pessimistic outlook.

1. Josie loves one son more than the other.
   Is this sad?

2. How does Josie feel about the way he treated Bobby Mahon?
   What does this tell you about human nature?

3. Does Josie have regrets in life?
   What does this add to the general vision and viewpoint?

4. Josie cannot bear talking to his daughter, and does not feel guilty about it.
   What is your response to this?
   How does this make you feel?

5. What made Josie undercut his former boss?
   What does Josie's story about the "big fat man from Cashel" show you about life?
   Is this a positive or negative comment on how people treat one another?

6. What made Josie give up drinking?
   What does this tell you about him?
   Is this a positive or negative comment on human nature?

7. How does Josie feel about what Pokey has done?
   How does he feel about Pokey?
   How does this make you feel?

8. Josie says, "We should have known it would all end in tears around here, it all started with tears…"

Comment on Josie's attitude and how it affects the outlook in this chapter.

# Relationships

Josie does not love his children equally, preferring his eldest son to Pokey and his daughter.

He describes a lifetime devoted to work rather than family, which leaves him regretful and adrift.

1. Describe Josie's relationships with his sons. How does he feel about them?

2. What sort of father was Josie when his children were growing up?

3. How does Josie feel about his daughter?

4. Why hasn't Josie told Eamonn what Pokey has done?

5. How does Pokey view Eamonn?

# Hero, Heroine, Villain

Josie thinks highly of Bobby Mahon and regrets how he treated him when Bobby came to speak to him. He was always glad to have Bobby to keep Pokey in check.

Josie thinks that Pokey was a bit afraid of Bobby, but in admiration of him too.

1. What does Josie think of Bobby Mahon?

2. How did Pokey view Bobby Mahon?

3. How does this chapter add to your view of Bobby?

# Chapter 3
# Lily

Lily is a prostitute. Her account reveals how she has been bady treated and looked down on because of this.

## Cultural Context/Social Setting

Lily's account shows the violence of this world. She is beaten by her baby's father, such is his rage and shame at being called the father of a prostitute's child. The police sergeant is glad when Lily does not report the assault. In this world, it is better to pretend that no assault happened, rather than seek justice for this woman who sells sex to men.

Lily is looked down upon in this society, even by the men who visit her. Her children are very ashamed of her, judging her harshly, as the community does.

1. Why did Bernie come and beat Lily?
   What does this tell you about this world?

2. Why is Jim Gildea, the sergeant, glad that Lily says she fell when he sees her face?
   What does this tell you about this world?

3. Why do men call to Lily?
   Does this help explain Bernie's treatment of her and Jim Gildea's reluctance to help?
   What does this tell you about the attitudes of people in this society?

4. Lily mentions refusing a good man, whose wife was expecting at the time.
   Who was this man?
   What does this reference tell you about this world?

5. Why don't Lily's children call to her?
   What does this tell you about this world?

6. "Imagine if they knew there's a solicitor inside in the city, the son of a whore, who's kin of theirs."
   How would the McDermotts react if they knew such a thing?
   What does this tell you about this world?

## Literary Genre

Lily's open, honest account adds another layer of understanding to the story's setting. The violence and scorn she has experienced are startling.

Her failed relationships with her children adds to the sad, regretful tone that connects each account.

1. Are you shocked by this chapter's opening section?
   What makes it shocking?

2. What does Lily's story about refusing a good man tell you about her character?
   What does this memory add to the narrative?

3. How does Lily's account add to the story?

# General Vision and Viewpoint

Lily's account opens with violence. The father of her fifth child assaults her before cutting her out of his life completely. She has been beaten by a man who is disgusted to be her baby's father. His violence and indifference to his child are negative comments on life, showing the pain people cause one another. The sergeant is happy not to investigate the matter, compounding Lily's bad treatment. The outlook here is very bleak in the face of such heartlessness and violence.

Lily's children want nothing to do with her. She neglected them as children, and now they are thoroughly ashamed of her. It is sad that their relationships are so damaged, and that her children cannot see past her sex work, but judge her harshly. However, Lily still loves them. She feels that she made her choices and lived her life, and there is worth in that.

1. Lily thought Bernie had come to see his child, when in fact he had come to beat and threaten her.
   How does this episode make you feel?
   Is this a positive or negative comment on life?

2. Jim Gildea, the sergeant, is glad that Lily lies about how she hurt her face.
   What is going on here?
   How does this make you feel?

3. Lily mentions refusing a good man once.
   What motivated her to refuse this man?
   Was this an act of kindness or spite?
   What does this suggest?

4. Lily's children never visit her.
Do you feel sorry for Lily?
Explain your point of view.

5. How did Bernie react when Lily said she had been with no-one but him for almost a year?
How does this make you feel?

6. Will Lily's children be sad when she dies?
How do they feel about her?
How do they treat her?
How does Lily's relationship with her children make you feel?
What does her relationship with her children suggest about lfe?

7. Is Lily disappointed with her life?
How does this add to the outlook?

## Relationships

This chapter involves violent and damaged, dysfunctional relationships. Lily describes being violently beaten by the father of her child. She thought he had come to see the baby, but instead he blackens her eye and knocks out her front tooth.

Now that she is older, Lily finds herself alone. Her children are ashamed of her and have little time for her.

1. How does Bernie react when he hears he is the father of Lily's child?

2. How do Lily's children treat her?
   Why do they treat her this way?

3. Describe Lily's relationship with John-John.
   What positives and negatives do you see?

4. What insight does Lily give into Bobby's relationship with his mother?

5. Was Lily a good mother to her children?
   Do you understand why her children feel cold towards her?

6. How did Bernie respond when Lily said he was the only one she had been with for nearly a year?
   What does this tell you about their relationship?

7. Lily financed her son through college, but was not invited to his graduation.
   What does this tell you about their relationship?

8. How does Lily feel about her children?
   How do her children feel about her?

9. What characterises Lily's relationships with others?
   How is she treated?

10. What do you notice about Lily's relationships?
    Are they positive or negative?
    Use examples to support your view.

## Hero, Heroine, Villain

Lily speaks highly of Bobby. He is friendly towards her and she sees nothing of his father in him. She remembers how upset he was when his mother died, weak from sadness and regret.

1. Does Lily have a good opinion of Bobby? Support your answer with quotation.

2. What does Lily add to your understanding of Bobby's character?

# Chapter 4
# Vasya

Vasya came to work in Ireland after his brother was beaten to death. He was one of Pokey Burke's workers. He cannot go home to his family after what happened to his brother.

## Cultural Context/Social Setting

Vasya's account gives an insight into what it is like to be an immigrant working on Irish building sites.

Vasya's memory of his brother's beating and death shows the violence of the world of the text, and explains why Vasya left home and came to be in Bobby's town.

The fact that Vasya can never go home, as he cannot face his parents after what happened his brother, shows how isolated Vasya is, and gives an insight into the rules of families that cannot be crossed.

1. How does Vasya describe the Irish countryside? What does he notice in particular?

2. How do you know that Vasya is not from Ireland?

3. How do you know that family is important to Vasya?

4. How is Vasya treated by the other men on site?

5. What does Vasya's experience in the unemployment office make clear?

6. What was it like for Vasya and his brother in the city?
What were their living and working conditions like?

7. What happened to Vasya's brother?
What does this reveal about this world?

8. Vasya explains that terms like "*off the books, under the table, on the queue tee*" helped him to find work.
What does this suggest about Irish employers?

9. What is stopping Vasya from going home?
What does this tell you about his family?

10. What differences can you see between Vasya's family home and where he lives now?

11. Where does Vasya live now?
Does he like it there, do you think?
What sort of life do these men have?

12. How does the man in 'The Miner's Rest' treat Vasya?
What does this tell you about Irish culture?

13. From what you have read so far, how do men behave in the world of the novel?
Why, do you think, do they behave this way?

## Literary Genre

Vasya's account adds another perspective to the narrative, that of someone who has come to work in the building trade in Ireland.

His backstory is one of poverty and the extremely violent death of his brother. This continues the sombre tone of previous chapters.

There is beauty in the lake imagery. Vasya's fear of swimming in the lake could symbolise his isolation; he is separate and adrift, without someone to help him. His description of getting lost as he walks the fields could also stand for the feeling of searching and not belonging that he feels.

1. What does Vasya's point of view as an immigrant labourer add to the story?

2. What does his backstory add to the narrative?

3. What does the image and description of the lake add to this chapter?

4. What does Vasya's story of walking the fields and getting lost add to the story?
   Is it symbolic in your view?

5. What does Vasya's account add to the story?

## General Vision and Viewpoint

The violent death of Vasya's brother and the isolation Vasya feels because of it darken the outlook here. Both the violent way that his brother died, and the fact that Vasya cannot return to his parents because of his brother's death, are very saddening and upsetting.

There is a note of optimism in the solace Vasya takes from having found a new home, and the beauty he sees in the world.

Pokey Burke's lying promise of paying Vasya shows how Pokey cheated his workers and left them with nothing, a dark comment on the selfishness of human nature as the chapter ends.

1. Why did Vasya and his brother go to the city?

2. What happened to Vasya's brother when they worked on a building site?
   How does this make you feel?

3. How did Vasya's brother die?
   What is your response to this?
   What does this demonstrate about human nature and life?

4. Why can Vasya never go home?
   How does this make you feel?

5. Is Vasya's future made bleak by the fact that he cannot go home?
   Fully explain your point of view.

6. Are people kind or cruel to Vasya?
   What does this suggest about life?

7. The chapter ends with Pokey Burke deceiving Vasya.
   How does this make you feel?
   Does this match the tone of earlier chapters?

# Relationships

Vasya cannot return home without his brother. Having lost him, he finds himself entirely isolated and alone. His parents would be disgusted by his return, so he must stay instead in Ireland. He has lost his brother, and because of their lack of understanding, his parents are lost to him too.

1. Does Vasya get on well with the other men on the building site?
   Do they like and respect him?

2. How were Vasya and his brother treated in the city?

3. What stopped Vasya from returning home from the city?

4. How was Vasya treated by Pokey Burke?

5. Describe Vasya's relationship with his parents.

# Hero, Heroine, Villain

Vasya describes Bobby as having a soft voice. He reminds Vasya of his father.

# Questions

1. How was Vasya treated by the foreman (Bobby)?
   How does this add to your understanding of Bobby's character?

# Chapter 5
# Réaltín

Réaltín lives in a ghost estate. She has no time for Seanie, her son Dylan's father.

Réaltín fancies Bobby when he comes to her house to do some work.

## Cultural Context/Social Setting

Réaltín lives in one of only two occupied houses in a ghost estate. Her home and surroundings embody the economic collapse and recession taking place.

Réaltín is not sure that Seanie is her son's father. She knows this would shock her father, which shows his traditional views. It also tells us that Réaltín has sexual freedom and choices that her father's generation did not.

Bobby's willingness to work for just fifty euro, and Réaltín's shortage of money, are reminders of the financial situation of the time, where money is scarce.

1. Réaltín lives in a ghost estate.
   What does this mean?

2. "I'm not sure if Seanie is even Dylan's father. Imagine if Daddy knew that!"
   What does Réaltín's comment reveal about the attitudes of her father's generation?

3. What do the fees George charged for conveyancing reveal about the property boom?

4. Réaltín mentions George's clients' violent crimes.
What does this remind you of?
What does it suggest about this world?

## Literary Genre

Réaltín sounds more defiant and hopeful than some of the other characters to date. The ghost estate she lives in is an effective symbol of the recession, a deserted, unfinished building site. Her recounting of sleeping with her boss and her friend Hillary's reaction adds humour to this chapter. Her interest in Bobby Mahon is significant as it will feature in local gossip later.

1. Do you get a good sense of the character of Réaltín's father here?
   How is this achieved?

2. What does Réaltín's story about having sex with her boss add to the narrative?

3. What is Réaltín's reaction to meeting Bobby Mahon?
   What, do you think, will happen here?

4. Does Réaltín really believe that having Bobby work for her will be a chore?
   What is she doing here?
   What does this add to the story?
   What does this suggest about her character?

5. Is there humour in Réaltín's chapter?
   What does this add to the story?

6. How is Réaltín's voice different to that of the other characters?
Use examples to explain what you mean here.

## General Vision and Viewpoint

Réaltín's father cares a lot about her, and she adores her son Dylan. This makes this chapter more positive and hopeful than others, despite Réaltín's unfortunate housing situation.

Although she has experienced loss, sadness, and financial difficulties, Réaltín has not been overcome by them. Her resilience adds positivity to the outlook here. She is a forward-looking character, and as the chapter ends, she is looking forward to seeing Bobby again.

1. How did the auctioneer mislead Réaltín?
What is your response to this?

2. Does Réaltín's father help and support her?
Is this a positive or negative aspect of her life?

3. How does Réaltín explain the way she was when meeting Seanie, and how she accidentally had sex with George?
How does this make you feel?

4. Does Réaltín have a positive or negative outlook on life?
Explain your view.

5. From what you have read so far, is life fair for characters?
What does this suggest about the author's view of life?

# Relationships

Réaltín's father is very attentive and caring, doing his best to look out for Réaltín and her son, Dylan.

Réaltín does not have much time for her father's partner, Bridget.

Réaltín thinks Seanie, Dylan's dad, is completely useless. She is not certain that he is Dylan's father, as she also had sex with her boss, George, around the time he was conceived.

Réaltín's mother died shortly before the period where she was seeing Seanie, and had sex with George. Réaltín was greatly affected by her mother's death, and it impacted on her relationships with others at the time.

1. Does Réaltín care about her father?

2. Does Réaltín depend on her father?

3. Does Réaltín's father care for her and Dylan? Use examples to support your ideas.

4. How does Réaltín feel about her son, Dylan?

5. What is stopping Réaltín from moving in with her father and Bridget?

6. How does Réaltín feel about her father's partner, Bridget?

7. Does Réaltín have a good relationship with Seanie? Explain your view.

8. What is Réaltín's first impression of Bobby Mahon?

9. Does Réaltín have a good relationship with her father? How does this father-child relationship compare with other father-child relationships in the novel?

10. Are Réaltín's relationships with others difficult or complicated?
Explain your view.

## Hero, Heroine, Villain

Réaltín describes Bobby as being handsome and manly.

He has come to check if her house has been properly finished. When she says it hasn't, and that she has no money to pay him, he kindly offers to do all the work for fifty euro.

1. How does Réaltín describe Bobby?

2. How does Bobby react when Réaltín says she has no money to pay him for working on her house?
What does this tell you about Bobby?

# Chapter 6
# Timmy

Timmy talks about Bobby, and how he stood up for Timmy on the site. He tells the unhappy story of his family.

## Cultural Context/Social Setting

Timmy says a lot of men are emigrating, but he is not.

He hopes to become a sacristan in the Church, showing that religion is important to him.

He speaks of his nana, who feared hospitals and mistrusted black doctors, who lived her whole life a short distance from where she was born. In his nana, Timmy captures an older Ireland, a smaller place that distrusted what it did not know. However, her outlook also stresses the positives of this rural place, the comfort of community and belonging.

Timmy's experience of working for Pokey, of being the butt of the men's jokes, shows the toxic, macho side of this working environment.

Timmy's upbringing was sad and difficult. His siblings were divided among relatives after his mother died and his father turned to drink. Reading of his childhood creates the impression of a difficult, uncaring world.

1. "A power of fellas is going foreign."
   What does Timmy mean here?

2. Is Timmy religious?
   Explain your view.

3. What do Nana's comments about hospitals reveal about her attitudes and outlook?

4. Timmy's nana "lived her whole life only over the road a small bit from the house she was born in."
What impression does this give you of this world?

5. What was Nana's attitude to motorcars?
What does this reveal about her outlook?

6. What does Mickey Briars complain that "years ago a fella starting off would've been sent all over the town" tell you about how new labourers are treated?

7. Timmy says Seanie Shaper showed him pictures of naked women and the men all laughed at him.
What was going on here?
What does this tell you about the world of these men?

8. Timmy's mother died in childbirth.
Does this surprise you?
What does this tell you about this world?

9. Who did Timmy and his siblings live with, growing up?
Why was this the case?
What does this tell you about this world?

10. Why does Peadar want to sell Nana's cottage?
What does this tell you about this world?

11. What does Timmy's job interview for the kitchen porter position tell you about the economic climate?

12. What picture are you forming of working on a building site in this world?
    Does it sound like it is friendly and fun, or difficult to deal with?

13. How do men treat each other in this world?
    What characterises the behaviour of men, from what you have read so far?
    What makes them behave as they do?

## Literary Genre

Timmy's nana's comments ground the story in its setting, reminding us of the old-fashioned, traditional views held by the older generation in many parts of the country.

Timmy speaks positively and warmly of Bobby. Through his eyes, the reader sees Bobby's kindness and strength of character. This overwhelmingly positive view of Bobby is being added to and built on in each chapter as our sense of him is developed.

Timmy's life story is saddening, and adds to the sombre atmosphere and tone of the novel.

1. Is there humour in this chapter?

2. What does Timmy add to your understanding of Bobby's character?

3. Consider the imagery in Timmy's story about the trip to the beach.
   What strikes you here?

4. What does the story of Noreen's baby add to the narrative?
   What is the mood like at this point?

5. What does Timmy contribute to your sense of the novel's setting?
   What does this add to the story?

## General Vision and Viewpoint

There is a lot of sadness in this chapter. Timmy is the butt of the building labourers' jokes, he lives a lonely life, and has had a sad childhood without his parents, separated from his siblings.

Timmy's account shows how difficult life can be, adding to the unhappy outlook of the novel.

1. Timmy says that stuff like skimming stones well only ever happens when there is nobody else there to see it. Comment on his outlook here.

2. What do Timmy's nana's attitudes add to the outlook? Was she a positive or negative person?

3. How does Mickey Briars and Seanie Shaper making fun of Timmy make you feel?

4. Are you glad that Bobby told Seanie to leave Timmy alone?

5. What was Timmy's childhood like?

6. How does the story of Noreen's baby make you feel?

7. What is Peadar's plan for Nana's cottage?
   What is his motivation here?
   Is he treating Timmy fairly?
   How does this make you feel?

8. Do you feel sorry for Timmy?
   Explain your view.

## Relationships

Timmy speaks highly of Bobby, who always treated him well, unlike the other men on site.

Timmy has a very poor relationship with his father, who abandoned him as a child and does not speak to him.

Timmy's sister has invited him to live with her, but he does not want to. She blames herself for her baby dying, thinking it is because she didn't mind Timmy when he was a child. He does not want her to be sad thinking about this.

Timmy emerges as a lonely, isolated figure. Although very much connected to his home place and in touch with his family, his relationships lack warmth, love and understanding.

1. How does Timmy know Bobby?
   How does he view him?

2. How did Bobby treat Timmy when he worked for Pokey Burke?
   Why is this significant?

3. Describe Timmy's relationship with his father.
   Is he similar to other characters in this regard?
   Use examples to support your view.

4. How did Noreen treat Timmy when her baby died?
   What was Timmy unsure about?
   What does this memory tell you about his relationship with his sister?

5. What are Peadar's views about Timmy inheriting Nana's cottage?
   Does Peadar care about Timmy, do you think?

6. Why doesn't Timmy want to live with Noreen?
   Does he care about his sister?
   Does she care about him?

7. Does Timmy have many positive relationships in his life?
   Use examples to support your view.

## Hero, Heroine, Villain

Bobby stood up for Timmy against Seanie Shaper and always treated him well. This reinforces the impression that Bobby is a just, decent man, who treats others with respect and is not afraid to involve himself when he sees someone being mistreated.

1. How did Bobby treat Timmy when they worked together?
   How does this add to your understanding of Bobby's character?

Does it make Bobby a more likeable character?
Explain your view.

2. What characteristics of Bobby's have been mentioned by different characters so far?
Are you building a positive or negative picture of him in your mind?
Explain your view.

# Chapter 7
# Brian

Brian has to emigrate to Australia to get work. He describes the impact his emigration is having on his life.

## Cultural Context/Social Setting

Brian has to emigrate as he has no employment opportunities at home. His mother is upset that he is leaving, while his father refuses to talk about it. In this society, men are reluctant to express themselves emotionally, keeping their feelings pent-up and unsaid.

When Brian's girlfriend breaks up with him, expecting him to be unfaithful in Australia, he denies that he is crying and does not talk to her about it. He claims that sex is all that men miss when they cry over women. This suggests a society where men cannot talk about their feelings, or see themselves as loving, emotional creatures.

Brian considers how he and his friends are so concerned about upsetting their parents. He wonders if it is because his actions will always affect them, realising the strength of family bonds in this society.

Brian fears that if he cries on the way to the airport, his friend Kenny will mock him and make jokes about him being a girl. This shows how men are shamed when expressing themselves emotionally, a culture of toxic masculinity. It also suggests that to be female is to be weak and overly-emotional, a sexist stereotype. In this world, both men and women suffer because of sexist attitudes.

Brian says Bobby Mahon is said to be having sex with a girl from town, showing that gossip and rumour are rife.

COMPARATIVE STUDY GUIDE • 45

1. How did Brian's parents view those emigrating to Australia a few years ago?
   Why is Brian emigrating?
   What has changed?

2. How are Brian's parents responding to the fact that Brian has to emigrate?
   What does this tell you about this world?

3. What does Brian's father's use of denial tell you about his attitudes?

4. "Dopey bitch. As if I'd cry over her."
   Describe Brian's attitude towards his girlfriend.

5. What does Brian's reaction to his break-up reveal about this culture?

6. What does Brian's reference to Kenny having drugs (Es) suggest about this world?

7. "We're all afraid of our lives of upsetting our parents."
   What does this tell you about values in this world?

8. "I'll be writing in a diary next, like a right prick"
   What do Brian's words here reveal?
   What comment is he making on his society?

9. If Brian cries, his friend, Kenny, will mock him and call him a girl.
   What does this tell you about how men and women are viewed and treated in this world?

10. Is Brian's family religious?

11. "He's meant to be tapping a flaker of a wan…"
What is Brian talking about?
What does this tell you about this community?

12. Brian calls Bobby a "proper man".
What is a 'proper man' in this world?

## Literary Genre

This chapter provides an insight into the issue of emigration. The author breathes life into this issue by making it personal. Through Brian, the reader realises the harsh reality of emigration for many young people in this world.

1. What does Brian's account make you realise about emigration?

2. Is there humour in this chapter?
Explain your view.

## General Vision and Viewpoint

Brian sees his emigration to Australia as a burden, calling himself a tragic figure and a victim. His parents are upset that he is leaving, feeling a sense of loss and injustice that their son is being forced to emigrate.

Brian's mother is fearful about him leaving, imagining all the troubles that may befall him, a very pessimistic outlook.

His girlfriend breaks up with him, expecting him to be unfaithful when he is away. He denies that he is upset about this, blaming his emotional upset on the fact that he is missing sex. He plans to come home in great shape, with lots of money, to spitefully show Lorna, his ex, what she has missed out on. Spite and revenge motivate Brian here, contributing to the negative outlook in this chapter.

Brian fears that if his father cries on the way to the airport, he will too, and then his friend will mock him. This shows how much he cares about his father, and how little his friend understands him or shows compassion.

Brian ends the chapter wishing to be Bobby Mahon. His unhappiness with himself adds to the sad tone in this account.

1. Brian says he is a "victim" because he is emigrating.
   Is this true?
   Do you feel sorry for him?

2. How are Brian's parents coping with the idea that he is emigrating?
   Are they upset?
   How does this make you feel?

3. Why does Lorna break up with Brian?
   What does this suggest about how she views him and their relationship?
   Is this a positive or negative attitude to have?

4. *"She'll* be crying the next time she sees me"
   Comment on Brian's attitude here.
   Does he sound spiteful to you?

5. "I wanted to be Bobby Mahon. I still do, imagine. I'm some loser. Why can't I want to be me?"

How is Brian feeling?
How does reading this make you feel?

6. Is Brian a happy character?
Explain your view.

## Relationships

Brian's relationships with his parents are strained due to him emigrating. His parents are unhappy about it. His mother worries about him, while his father won't talk about it, which Brian finds difficult, as it makes him feel guilty.

Brian's girlfriend broke up with him, expecting him to be unfaithful in Australia. He claims not to care about the break-up, saying it is just sex that he misses. He wants to have sex with an attractive blonde and come home tanned and rich to spite Lorna. His wish to get revenge and spite her suggests that the break-up has hurt him more then he says.

An inability to speak openly and emotionally characterises Brian's relationships.

1. How do Brian's parents feel about him emigrating?

2. Why does Brian find his father's silence about him going to Australia so difficult?
What does this tell you about his relationship with his father?

3. Why has Brian's girlfriend broken up with him?
What does this suggest about their relationship?

4. How did Brian react when his girlfriend broke up with him?
   What does this tell you?

5. "As if I'd cry over her."
   Is Brian in denial here?
   Explain your view.

6. Does Brian care about Lorna, do you think?
   Use examples to support your ideas.

7. What will the drive to the airport be like?
   What does this reveal to you about Brian's relationship with his parents?
   What does this reveal to you about Brian's parents' relationship?

8. What will Brian do if he sees his father crying?
   What does this tell you about how he feels about his father?

9. Is a lot left unsaid in this world?
   What does this tell you about these characters' relationships?

## Hero, Heroine, Villain

Brian calls Bobby a proper man. He admires the way he carries himself, as if he has nothing to prove, and looks up to him for being tough.

1. Does Brian admire Bobby?
   How do you know?

2. What does Brian's view of Bobby add to your impression of Bobby Mahon?

# Chapter 8
# Trevor

Trevor's dark account reveals his obsession with Réaltín and his plans to kidnap her son and frame and kill his mother.

## Cultural Context/Social Setting

Trevor appears to have mental health problems, and has not sought help. He has not found out whether schizophrenia is hereditary. Avoiding information about his father's mental illness may suggest a society lacking in understanding of mental health problems.

Dorothy gossips about Réaltín, thinking her father must be ashamed of her and her bastard child. Dorothy reveals the gossiping, judgemental nature of this world.

Trevor's plans of kidnapping and murder show that this place can be unpredictable, dangerous and frightening.

1. Trevor says that his father was schizophrenic.
   What does this term mean?

2. Trevor does not want to find out if schizophrenia is hereditary.
   Comment on his attitude here.
   What does it reveal about his world?

3. Dorothy says that Réaltín's father must be ashamed of her.
   What two reasons does she give for this shame?

What does her attitude tell you about this world and how women are viewed and treated?

4. "There's no knowing what way she pays him for his work."
What is Dorothy suggesting here?
Comment on her attitude.

5. Trevor says that "there aren't many respectful men in the world."
What does this tell you about how he views the behaviour of men where women are involved?
Does he accept or oppose this behaviour?

# Literary Genre

Trevor appears as a threatening, dangerous character in this chapter, which adds anticipation and excitement to the story.

His plans to kill his mother and her friend Dorothy, after pinning the kidnap of Réaltín's son on them, adds tension and suspense.

Trevor is a menacing, unstable character, and his plans to commit harm add pace and excitement to the plot.

1. What are your first impressions of Trevor?
What strikes you about him?

2. Comment on the imagery when Trevor imagines killing Dorothy.

3. What does Trevor's fixation with "that girl" (Réaltín) add to the story?

4. Is Trevor a dangerous or threatening character?
What creates this impression?
Be specific in your answer.

5. Dorothy suspects that there is something going on between Bobby and Réaltín.
Is this likely, based on what you know of Bobby's character?
Use examples to support your view.

6. Is the information Trevor gives us in this chapter reliable? How does his chapter add to the story?

7. Is this an exciting chapter?
Support your view with reference to the story.

8. What adds tension in this chapter?
Be specific in your answer.

## General Vision and Viewpoint

This is a very dark chapter. Trevor and his mother have a flawed, destructive relationship. She criticises him, while he plots to kill her.

Trevor is convinced that he is ill and about to die.

He is obsessed with the girl from the ghost estate.

Trevor's outlook is dark and violent. He speaks of evil and believes that his mother is a witch. His instability and plans of kidnapping and murder make this a very dark account.

1. What is your response to the way Trevor's mother speaks to him about his sunglasses?

2. "I'm dying. I'm sure of it."
   Describe Trevor's outlook here.

3. Trevor imagines killing Dorothy.
   What does this add to the mood at this point?

4. What accusations does Trevor make about his mother?
   Comment on his outlook here.

5. What plans is Trevor making?
   What do they tell you about his outlook?
   How do you feel, reading about what he plans to do?

6. Is there a sense of danger or threat in this chapter?
   How is this feeling created?
   What does it add to the general vision and viewpoint?

7. How do you feel as the chapter ends?

## Relationships

This account portrays another very flawed parent-child relationship. Trevor's mother appears to be hard on him, expecting him to disappoint her. He describes his mother as evil, and thinks she is trying to drive him mad. He outlines his plan to frame her for kidnapping, and kill her for being a witch.

Although Trevor describes her as evil, when she discovers him slumped forward in his chair, his mother is very concerned about him.

Trevor is fixated with the girl from the ghost estate and fantasises about her. He imagines murdering her neighbour and having Réaltín rush into his arms. His obsession with Réaltín is a fantasy, without any grounding in reality.

1. What are your first impressions of Trevor's relationship with his mother?
   Use examples to support your view.

2. Trevor imagines killing Dorothy and "that girl"rushing into his arms.
   What is his relationship to Réaltín?
   Does Trevor have a good understanding of how relationships work, do you think?

3. How does Trevor view his mother?
   What does this tell you about their relationship?
   What makes him feel this way about her?

4. What different things does Trevor accuse his mother of?

5. What does Trevor plan to do to his mother?
   What does this tell you about how he views her and feels about her?

6. How does Trevor's mother react when she discovers him slumped forward?
   What does this tell you about how she feels sbout him?

7. There are rumours about Bobby and Réaltín.
   Do you think Bobby is having an affair behind his wife's

back?
Use examples to support your view.

# Hero, Heroine, Villain

Trevor is suspicious of Bobby's relationship with Réaltín. He describes Bobby as handsome, and assumes he is taking advantage of Réaltín.

It is significant that Trevor does not know Bobby personally, he has just heard Dorothy's gossip. His views are based on rumour and his own fantasy.

1. How does Trevor describe Bobby?

2. What sort of person does Trevor imagine Bobby to be?

3. Does Bobby having an affair fit in with your view of his character?
Fully explain your point of view.

# Chapter 9
# Bridie

Bridie's sad account centres around the story of her son's drowning and how it has affected her.

## Cultural Context/Social Setting

Bridie's story of her son's drowning adds to the picture of this place as one of loss and sadness.

Bridie mentions losing her job, adding to the idea that work is hard to come by here.

She mentions embarrassing her husband by shouting at the parish priest, showing how important a figure the priest is in their community.

Bridie describes the "coven of auld bitches" gossiping in the post office, showing how vicious and vibrant gossip and rumour are here.

Bridie remembers taking in Bobby and his mother one time when Frank was drunkenly destroying the furniture in their cottage. Her actions here show the caring, compassionate side of this community, and how people help one another.

1. How did Bridie lose her job?

2. Bridie mentions the *"current climate"*. What does she mean here?

3. Why did Bridie's husband apologise when Bridie told the priest where to go?

Is the priest looked up to in this society?
How do you know?

4. What does Bridie's description of the gossiping women in the post office queue tell you about this place?

5. Why did Michael want the blocks for the sunroom delivered early?
What does this tell you about this community?

6. Bridie took Bobby and his mother in once when Frank was drunk and destroying the furniture in their cottage. What do Bridie's actions here show you about this world?

7. What stopped Bobby's mother from leaving Frank, in your opinion?

## Literary Genre

This chapter highlights personal loss and sorrow, adding to the sense of sadness running through these accounts. Bridie speaks of the death of her son and the impact this loss had on her life. She turned her back on the church, and on county Clare, due to her grief and sorrow.

Consider how the author is framing the idea of a mother's grief here, clearly depicting the harrowing effect of her son's loss on her. This is foreshadowing, laying context for the kidnapping plot strand that is emerging.

Bridie reminds us of Bobby's dysfunctional relationship with his father, Frank, and the sadness it has caused him. In this way, this theme remains to the fore of the reader's mind.

1. Comment on the imagery where Bridie thinks about her son's death.
   What does it add to the story here?

2. Do you get a clear insight into Bridie's character in this chapter?
   How is this achieved?

3. The question of whether Bobby is having an affair has surfaced again.
   What does this add to the story?

4. What themes or central ideas in the novel does Bridie's chapter reinforce and strengthen?

## General Vision and Viewpoint

Bridie's story of her son's drowning is sad and moving. She remembers the drive to the search party as the last time she had hope. The fact that his body was never recovered compounds her sadness, adding to the sorrowful tone and sense of loss here.

She explains how Peter's drowning changed her. She is short-tempered and judgemental now in a way she never was before. Her bad humour and short temper have impacted negatively on her relationships with her children, another saddening fact.

The outlook here is sad and bleak as Peter's death was a heartbreaking event Bridie never recovered from. It also led to the breakdown of her marriage, adding to her isolation and damaged relationships.

Bridie's recounting of Bobby's sadness on seeing his father further demonstrates the negative relationships in this text and the sadness they bring to characters' lives.

Bridie's kindness in having once taken in Bobby and his mother reminds us of the goodness in people. She did not embarrass them, but treated them compassionately when they were in need. This provides a glimmer of light and hope in a dark, sad chapter.

1. Why does Bridie hate county Clare?
   How does this contribute to the mood here?

2. What does Bridie think of when she thinks about her son?
   How does this make you feel?

3. How does reading Bridie's account of looking for her son make you feel?

4. Bridie says she has no hope now.
   What does this tell you about her outlook?

5. How did her son's death impact on Bridie's marriage?
   How does this make you feel?

6. How has Peter's drowning impacted on Bridie as a person?
   How does this make you feel?

7. How does Bridie's account of Bobby's strained relationship with his father add to the general vision and viewpoint here?

8. What does Bridie's memory of taking in Bobby and his mother show you about people and life?
   Is this a positive or negative comment on human nature?

9. "Life isn't fair, as the fella says"
Does this sum up Bridie's outlook?
Explain your point of view.

## Relationships

Bridie has poor relationships with her children and her marriage has broken down, all as a result of the impact of Peter's death on her.

Bridie remembers a sadness coming over Bobby one time on seeing his father. We are reminded of the gulf between these characters.

This chapter draws attention to the sadness and personal hurt that comes with damaged relationships.

## Questions

1. How does Bridie feel about her son's death?
   How has it affected her?
   How has it affected her marriage?

2. How does Bridie treat her children?
   Include examples to support your view.

3. Who does Bridie blame for Peter's death?

4. How has Peter's death impacted on Bridie's relationships with others?

5. How did Bobby react when he saw his father while delivering blocks to Bridie's?
What does this tell you about their relationship?

6. What insight does Bridie give into relationships in the Mahon household?

## Hero, Heroine, Villain

Bridie wonders if Bobby is having an affair, but does not want to think it is true. She draws attention to Bobby's poor relationship with his father.

1. What rumours are there about Bobby?

2. Does Bridie believe these rumours?

3. What does Bridie think of Bobby?

# Chapter 10
# Jason

Jason says that Bobby Mahon killed his father. His account is troubled and violent.

## Cultural Context/Social Setting

Jason describes a cruel, violent world; he was abused as a child and witnessed a shooting. His experience of this place is that it is harsh and violent.

Jason has a poor view of women, viewing the woman in the tattoo parlour as a sexual object. He also speaks of "slappers" being given housing. This derogatory tone highlights how women are viewed here. He says he should have "slapped the head off" his son's mother so he could see his child. Women are often the targets of violence in this world.

1. "I have no problem telling the cops stuff about a lad that'd do his own father in."
   What does this tell you about Jason's moral code?
   What does this suggest about the values of his society?

2. How have Jason's facial tattoos impacted on his life?
   What does this tell you about the society he lives in?

3. What does Jason's childhood tell you about this world?

4. What insight does the story about Eugene and the farmer give you into this world?

5. How does Jason view the assistant in the tattoo parlour? What does this tell you about how women are viewed and treated in this world?

6. "Them apartments they give to slappers do be fair nice." What is Jason talking about here? What does his use of the word "slapper" suggest?

7. "I should have bursted in through the door and slapped the head off her." What do Jason's words demonstrate to you about this world?

8. What impact has Frank's murder had on the community?

## Literary Genre

Jason begins his account by casually announcing that Bobby Mahon has killed his father. This is a very dramatic plot development. We know how much Bobby hated his father, but the idea that our likeable, well-respected protagonist has murdered his father is shocking. This forces the reader to think over all that has occurred to date in the story, to decide whether or not we believe Jason.

Jason mentions seeing a man in the vicinity at the time of the murder, introducing doubt and intrigue. The pace has changed here, there is a mystery to be solved.

Jason's chapter deals with a lot of violence and sadness. It is fitting that Frank's murder should be included in such a chapter.

1. Read the opening line of this chapter again.
   What is your response to this?

2. Is Jason a reliable witness?
   What does this bring to the story?

3. Is this an exciting chapter?
   Explain your view.

4. Is Jason an interesting character?
   Explain your view.

5. "A sort of a cold wave came off that auld fella."
   How does Jason describe Frank?
   Why has the author included this depiction of Frank at this point?

6. The chapter ends wth a very positive story about Bobby Mahon.
   Why has the author ended the chapter like this?

7. Is there humour in this chapter?
   If so, what does it add to the story?

8. Do you think Bobby has killed his father?
   Give reasons for your answer.

# General Vision and Viewpoint

Jason's account is dark and troubling, showing how difficult and harsh life can be. Jason was sexually abused as a child and witnessed a shooting, both of which have affected his mental health and wellbeing. He also has a child he does not see, but would like to, adding to his dissatisfaction with life.

Jason tells us that Bobby has killed his father, adding to the darkness snd bleak outlook of this chapter.

1. What sort of life has Jason had? How does this affect the general vision and viewpoint of this chapter?

2. How was Jason treated by his son's mother?

3. What happened with Jason, Eugene and the farmer?

4. What is your view of life, after reading this chapter?

5. Is this an easy account to read or is it upsetting? Give reasons for your answer.

## Relationships

Jason has experienced a lot of negative, destructive relationships. He was abused as a child, which has affected him greatly. His son's mother seems to have used him as a means to get pregnant and then rejected him, also adding to the negative relationships in this chapter.

Jason mentions violence in his relationships, accepting it as a normal way to deal with people.

Overall, Jason's chapter is a negative comment on relationships.

1. Describe Jason's relationship with the mother of his son. Is this a positive or negative relationship?

2. Are Jason's relationships with others generally positive or negative?
   Use examples to support your view.

3. What characterises Jason's relationships?
   Include examples to support your view.

4. Does Jason have a good relationship with Bobby Mahon? How does he view him?
   What does this suggest about Bobby's relationships and how he treats others?

## Hero, Heroine, Villain

Jason tells us that Bobby has killed his father. Although he thinks Bobby is a murderer, Jason still thinks that he is a sound character. Jason did not like Frank Mahon, and understands why Bobby might want to kill him.

Jason ends the chapter with an instance of Bobby's understanding and kindness, when he replaced a wheel on Jason's father's car, showing him in a positive light.

1. "I know in my heart and soul it was Bobby Mahon."
   What crime is Bobby guilty of, according to Jason?
   What is your response to this?

2. What is Jason's view of Bobby, despite the alleged murder?

3. What does Jason's story about the wheel tell you about Bobby?

# Chapter 11
# Hillary

Hillary complains about her friend Réaltín, and talks about Réaltín's interest in Bobby Mahon.

## Cultural Context/Social Setting

Hillary's chapter shows how prevalent gossip is in this world. She talks about how the older women in work treat her because they know about what happened between Réaltín and their boss.

She describes how upset Réaltín was to hear the gossip about her and Bobby. Gossip and rumour are vicious, and they are everywhere, it seems, in this world.

Hillary's additional work duties, and the idea that she should be grateful just to have work, reinforces the impression of this as a place with poor employment opportunites.

1. What insight does Hillary give you into her workplace? What does this tell you about her world?

2. What did Bridget hear about Réaltín? How did Réaltín react to this rumour? What does this tell you about this world?

3. "...the whole crazy village thinks she's a brazen, home-wrecking hussy..."
What insight does this give you into the type of place this

village is?
What values and attitudes are evident here?

4. Why were Réaltín and Hillary told that they would have to take a massive pay-cut?
What does this tell you about this world?

5. "Aren't you lucky to have a job?"
Explain what this shows about this world.

6. What does the cleaning rota reveal to you about this world?

7. Is this a very harsh, unfeeling place?
Give reasons for your answer.

## Literary Genre

Hillary adds to the exciting affair storyline. She gives an insight into how Réaltín feels about Bobby and the lengths she goes to to have reasons for him to call to her house. However, she says that nothing has happened between them, contradicting local gossip.

1. How does Hillary further the affair plot strand?
What information does she provide?

2. Is this piece very conversational?
How does Hillary draw the reader in?

3. How does Hillary view Bobby?
   What does she suggest he is capable of?
   Does she change your view of Bobby?

4. Is Hillary's account very sensational?
   Explain your view.
   What does this bring to the story?

## General Vision and Viewpoint

Hillary says she thinks highly of Réaltín, yet she lacks compassion for her friend, offering judgement instead. Hillary feels Réaltín draws on sadness, somehow blaming her for the sorrow and upset in her life, an approach lacking warmth or feeling.

Hillary wonders at Bobby secretly being a murderer all along, a dark and unsettling thought.

Hillary feels that Réaltín is self-centred and does not take a real interest in Hillary's problems. This shows the struggle that each of these characters must bear, largely alone. Life is shown to be difficult, and lonely.

1. "She's going to have to decide what she's doing with her life and stop being such a disaster."
   Is this a positive comment about Réaltín?
   How does it add to the outlook here?

2. "...and all that time there was a murderer hiding inside in him."
   Is this a very dark idea?
   What does it suggest about people?

3. According to Hillary, what else is Bobby capable of?
How does this affect the outlook?

4. Is Hillary sympathetic towards Réaltín being visited by the gardaí?
Is she unkind here?
Do you have sympathy for Réaltín?

5. Is Hillary a good friend to Réaltín?
How does this affect the general vision and viewpoint?

6. What problems does Hillary have in her own life?
What does this tell you about people and life?

## Relationships

Hillary is Réaltín's work colleague and friend, but does not have much sympathy for her. She focuses on Réaltín's faults and shortcomings and complains about her. Hillary feels that Réaltín is self-centred and does not take a real interest in what is going on in Hillary's life.

1. What is Hillary's relationship to Réaltín?
What is her view of Réaltín?

2. According to Hillary, what is Réaltín's relationship to Bobby?
Is she being entirely fair here?

3. Is Hillary a good friend to Réaltín?
Use examples to support the points that you make.

Does she value this friendship?
Support your view.

4. Is Réaltín a good friend to Hillary?
What does this tell you about their relationship?

## Hero, Heroine, Villain

Hillary says that nothing has happened between Bobby and Réaltín, despite Réaltín's best efforts. This contradicts earlier rumours and re-establishes our faith in Bobby's loyalty to Triona.

1. Hillary says that nothing has happened between Bobby and Réaltín.
Does this surprise you?

2. Does Hillary trust Bobby Mahon?
Does this change your view of him?
Give reasons for your answer.

# Chapter 12
# Seanie

Seanie talks about women and his relationship with Réaltín. He also mentions his depression, which he keeps secret.

## Cultural Context/Social Setting

Seanie's views towards women are sexist. He sees women as sexual objects.

However, in this world, although women are treated in a sexist way, they are not dependant on men, and are free to make their own choices. Réaltín chooses to be with Seanie, and then loses interest in him. She is free to break up with him and have other relationships. This suggests a certain freedom for women, despite the sexist culture evident in the novel.

Seanie is feeling very low, suffering from depression. He has not told anyone about this, choosing to keep it a secret. His silence here suggests that this is not a world where men can discuss their feelings or reveal any vulnerability that could be considered a weakness, forcing Seanie to bear his depression unsupported and alone.

1. What does Seanie's piece about nicknames tell you about this place?

2. Describe Seanie's attitude towards women.

3. What does Seanie's story about first seeing Réaltín tell you about this world?

4. Why didn't Seanie say much about Réaltín moving out here?

5. Seanie says he never told anyone about his depression. Why is this the case?
What does this tell you about this world?

6. How does Seanie's account add to your understanding of how women are viewed and treated in this society?

## Literary Genre

On a superficial level, Seanie appears to be a shallow, sexist character. His treatment of women casts him in a negative light. However, the author adds depth and detail concerning Seanie's sense of self to create a more rounded, complex character. When he speaks of his depression, and his feelings towards Réaltín and Dylan, another character emerges.

In this way, Ryan continues to suggest that each of his speakers has many facets to their character.

Seanie's searingly honest account adds to the confessional style of the story as he too reveals his secret self.

1. What is your initial impression of Seanie Shaper?
Does this view change throughout the chapter?
How does this add to the storytelling?

2. What is the mood like as this chapter ends?

3. What does the lake at the end of the chapter symbolise for Seanie?
   What does this add to the story?

4. How does the author add depth and complexity to Seanie's character?

## General Vision and Viewpoint

There is a sense of sadness and loss in Seanie's account. Seanie speaks of how easy it is to become depressed when life does not follow the path you thought it held for you. Seanie suffers from depression and feels very negatively about himself. He keeps his suffering to himself for fear of how he will be judged, a saddening note in the chapter. He feels like he has let his parents down and been a constant disappointment to them. His poor relationship with Réaltín and lack of contact with his son is a cause of sorrow for his parents, and Seanie feels bad about this.

Seanie ends his chapter with a story about women dying by drowning in a local lake. This dark image symbolises Seanie's depression, his hopelessness and the depth of his despair. It suggests that his outlook is bleak and hopeless, and that for him life is a struggle, full of difficulty and disappointment.

1. What is Seanie's attitude towards women?
   Is this a positive or negative comment on life?
   Explain your view.

2. Does Seanie have a good relationship with Réaltín?
   Do you feel sorry for Seanie here?

3. What do Seanie's words about depression tell you about life?

4. "He took on a rake of Polish subbies and screwed the poor pricks and we all thought it was a laugh."
Comment on this attitude and what it reveals about people and life.

5. How does Seanie feel about himself?
How does he view his own life?

6. How does Seanie's relationship with Réaltín and Dylan affect his happiness?

7. How does reading of Seanie's depression make you feel?

8. Is life a struggle for Seanie?
Fully explain your point of view.

9. How does reading the end of this chapter make you feel?

10. Does Seanie have a very bleak outlook?
Explain your view.

11. What does Seanie wish as the chapter ends?
How does this make you feel?

12. Is love possible for Seanie, do you think?
How does this make you feel?

## Relationships

Seanie's relationships have brought him sadness. He feels that his poor relationship with Réaltín and lack of contact with his son is a source of sadness and disappointment for his parents. He feels he has let them down, when they have done so much for him.

Seanie feels that he always gets things wrong with Réaltín. He knows that he says and does the wrong things, further worsening their relationship.

1. How did Seanie feel about Réaltín when they first started seeing each other?

2. How did Seanie's relationship with Réaltín develop?

3. How does Seanie feel about his son?
   Is he a good father?
   Use examples to support your view.

4. How does Seanie feel about his parents?

5. Does Seanie communicate his feelings well to others? How does this affect his relationships?

6. Does Seanie have good relationships with the important people in his life?
   Why is this the case?

## Hero, Heroine, Villain

Seanie thought that Bobby had been having sex with Réaltín, but says that

Bobby denied everything and said Seanie could believe what he liked. This suggests that Bobby does not care what people are saying about him.

Seanie also says that Bobby is devoted to his wife, Triona, saying that Bobby was the only one of them who always went home after work.

1. How does Seanie view Bobby?

2. What details does this chapter add to your understanding of Bobby's character?

# Chapter 13
# Kate

Kate talks about problems running her creche.

## Cultural Context/Social Setting

Kate recounts the financial difficulties she weathered when Dell closed. Her treatment of her workers shows they are not valued, she views them as being beneath her. She treats Nuala's challenges with contempt, seeing Nuala's work requests as annoyance rather than her responsibility as an employer. Her chapter gives an insight into difficulties in the workplace in this world, where work is hard to come by.

1. What impact did Dell closing have on Kate?
   What does this tell you about her world?

2. How does Kate manage to pay less than the minimum wage?
   What does this tell you about this world?

3. "Denis thinks I'm mad for taking on a *fella* as a Montessori teacher."
   What does this attitude reveal to you?

4. What does Kate say about men working together?
   What does this tell you about this society?

5. What does Kate checking her employees' Facebook pages tell you about how she views them?

6. Does Kate treat her workers well?
   In general, how are workers treated in this novel?
   Use examples to support your ideas.
   What does this tell you about attitudes and values in this world?

## Literary Genre

Kate mentions that Trevor applied for a job shortly after Réaltín visited. This reminds us of Trevor's obsession with Réaltín, adding tension.

She mentions her husband Denis' horrible father, and the fact that Denis must have had an awful time growing up. This echoes Bobby's upbringing, and keeps the theme of relationships in focus, without mentioning the main character himself.

1. How do you feel about Trevor applying for a job here, shortly after Réaltín called in?
   What does this add to the story?

2. Where do you see conflict in this chapter?
   What does it add to the story?

## General Vision and Viewpoint

What appears at first to be optimism on Kate's part materialises more clearly as spite as her chapter progresses. She looks down on her employees and rubbishes the idea that they have any rights or entitlements.

She is also harsh when speaking about her husband, Denis.

Kate's account suggests that life is hard, and that her workers need to be kept in line, in their proper place. There is little love or joy in her representation of life.

1. "You can't give your time whingeing and blaming, you have to just fight back."
   Describe Kate's outlook here.
   Does she have a positive or negative way of looking at things?

2. Does Kate have a difficult life?
   Explain your view.

3. How does Kate treat her workers?
   How does this make you feel?

4. What does Kate's dream reveal about her feelings towards Denis and Nuala?

5. Is Kate a positive or negative character?
   What does she contribute to the view of life offered in the novel?

## Relationships

Kate feels that Denis resents the success she has made of her creche business. They do not talk about the creche, he pretends it does not exist. Kate says he is very sensitive and that they have not had sex in four months.

Kate has an antagonistic relationship with her employee, Nuala, where they try to score points off one another. Kate checks up on her employees' Facebook pages, showing she does not trust them.

1. Does Kate have a good relationship with her staff? Explain your point of view.

2. Does Kate have a good relationship with Denis? Include examples to support your view.

3. Does Kate get on well with Nuala? Include examples to support your view.

4. What does Kate say about Denis' father? What does this add to the theme of relationships?

5. How did Kate react the last time Denis tried it on with her? What does this tell you about their relationship? How did Denis respond to her reaction? What does this tell you about their relationship?

6. What does Kate's dream suggest about how she feels about Denis and Nuala?

## Hero, Heroine, Villain

Bobby Mahon is not mentioned in this chapter.

# Chapter 14
# Lloyd

Lloyd explains that Trevor wanted his help to kidnap a kid and talks about his inner warrior's desire to kill the boy. Lloyd is a solipsist. (This means he is only sure of his own existence, he thinks everything else may be merely something he has thought up.)

## Cultural Context/Social Setting

Lloyd's mother is horrified to see his bong, which tells us she does not approve of his drug use. However, she does not broach the topic with Lloyd, choosing not to say anything about it, an avoidance that is characteristic of this world.

Trevor and Lloyd's kidnapping of Dylan shows that this world can be a dark, frightening and dangerous place. Lloyd knows that he has broken the law, and could be in real trouble, but shows no sign of acting on this knowledge. The law is ineffective here. Lloyd will determine what happens to Dylan, showing this world is a threatening, chaotic place.

1. How does Lloyd know Trevor?
   What does this tell you about this world?

2. How does Lloyd's mother react to seeing his bong?
   What does her reaction tell you about the attitudes of her society?

3. Lloyd and Trevor have kidnapped Dylan, and Lloyd is holding him captive.

What does this reveal to you about this world?

Are you shocked that such a thing could happen here?

## Literary Genre

There is tension in this chapter as Lloyd reveals that he has helped Trevor to kidnap Réaltín's son, Dylan. Lloyd speaks of his dream of killing the boy, saying it is what his inner self wants to do. This threat adds danger and menace to the chapter, making it very tense indeed.

Lloyd does not believe in the reality of the world, saying that nothing exists outside his consciousness. This insight into his mindset adds tension to this chapter. For Lloyd, killing Dylan would not be murder, as he does not believe that the boy is real. His impaired judgement adds threat and tension, as Dylan is in real danger.

Kidnapping, and the theme of losing a child, have already been mentioned in earlier chapters, preparing the reader for this development. The mood is dark and tense at this point in the story. As readers, we fear for Dylan's safety and want to know what happens next.

1. What does Trevor want Lloyd to help him with?
   What is your response to this?

2. "I dreamt I killed the kid."
   What is your response to reading Lloyd's dream?
   Does it make you feel worried or anxious?
   Explain your view.

3. "Then I woke up and the kid was standing up..."
   What is your response to this?

4. How is Lloyd interpreting this dream?
   What is your response to this?

5. What hints in the novel have suggested this kidnapping?
   Does it fit in well to the storyline?
   Explain your point of view.

6. Does anything in this chapter make you feel uneasy?
   Be precise in your answer.

7. "I don't think he knows he doesn't really exist as an entity independent of me."
   How does this insight into Lloyd's mindset affect the story here?
   How do you feel at this point?

8. Is Lloyd a thoroughly bad character?
   Explain your point of view.

9. How do you feel as the chapter ends?
   What, specifically, makes you feel this way?

## General Vision and Viewpoint

Lloyd and Trevor have done something very disturbing by kidnapping Dylan. Their actions suggest that the world is a dangerous, threatening place, where children are vulnerable and open to harm. Their actions are very troubling and upsetting, adding darkness, menace and a suggestion of violence to the novel's outlook.

1. How does Lloyd treat his mother?
   How does this make you feel?

2. How does Lloyd's story of his dad leaving when he was a child impact on the mood of this chapter?

3. Why is it significant that Lloyd's dad had another son? Explain the impact this had on Lloyd.

4. Lloyd and Trevor have kidnapped Réaltín's son.
   Is this a dangerous situation?
   How does this make you feel?
   What does this suggest about life?

## Relationships

Lloyd describes having a dream where he kills the boy. He believes this dream is an expression of an inner desire of his. He believes that he is the creator of his own universe and as such, no-one else is real, but is a facet of himself. This means that his relationships with others are stunted by their unreality, but are also very complex in Lloyd's eyes. His belief that no-one else is real means he cannot be concerned by how he may harm others, making him a potentially dangerous and destructive force.

1. How does Lloyd know Trevor?
   What is the basis of their relationship?

2. What are your first impressions of Lloyd's relationship with his mother?
   Does he treat her well?

3. What does Lloyd's parents' break-up add to the theme of relationships?

4. Lloyd says that his creations need to feel inferior to him and fearful of him.
   Does this add to your understanding of his interactions with others?
   How does Lloyd view others?

5. Do Trevor and Lloyd get on well together?
   Explain your view.

6. Are you surprised that Lloyd slaps Trevor in the face?

7. Are the relationships in this chapter generally positive or negative?
   Explain your view.

## Hero, Heroine, Villain

Bobby Mahon is not mentioned in this chapter. However, Lloyd emerges as a very threatening, dangerous character. His belief that no-one else is real adds an extra element of danger and threat to him. He is a 'bad' character, in complete contrast to Bobby Mahon.

1. Is Lloyd the opposite to Bobby?
   Explain your point of view.

# Chapter 15
# Rory

Rory rubbishes the rumours about Bobby and Réaltín. He says Jim Gildea found Bobby with his father's body, and a length of timber in his hand. Rory mentions meeting a girl he likes, but will not pursue, because he is sure he will mess it up.

## Cultural Context/Social Setting

Rory is considering emigrating to London. He cannot get work and is signing on for the dole. Leaving his parents is what is holding him back, showing how highly he values family.

When Rory describes the girl he meets at the gig poster, he begins with her "tits", and ends with her "lovely arse". This shows how women are viewed by men in this world, they are seen as sexual objects.

Rory speaks of the problem of thinking about things. He knows he will not go to the gig in town, for fear of making a fool of himself. Like other men in this world, he has a private world of sadness that he keeps unexpressed and hidden from others.

1. Rory has not contacted Bobby since he got out on bail. What does this tell you about this world?

2. Rory says, "Bobby must have finally had enough of his shit."
   Is Frank's murder acceptable in this world?
   Fully explain your point of view.

3. Where will Rory find work without Bobby to employ him?

4. What state is the country in, according to people in the community?

5. What is preventing Rory from going to London? What does this tell you about family in this world?

6. How does Rory describe the girl at the gig poster in town? What does the language he uses tell you about how women are viewed in this world?

7. What does Rory mentioning Father Cotter, and how seriously Rory took his advice, tell you about this world?

## Literary Genre

Rory spends a lot of time working with Bobby. His account provides some details surrounding the circumstances of Frank's murder, and so the murder storyline once again takes centre stage.

Rory admires Bobby, viewing him as a natural leader. Seeing Bobby through Rory's eyes inclines the reader to think well of him and admire him too.

1. How do Rory's parents feel about Bobby Mahon?

2. Rory provides some details surrounding the circumstances of Frank's murder. What does this add to the story?

3. Do these details sway your view of Bobby's guilt or innocence?
   Do you think he murdered his father?
   Support your answer with reference to the text.

4. Where do you see conflict in this chapter?
   What does it add to the story?

5. Does Rory add to your view of Bobby Mahon in this chapter?
   What details stand out for you?
   Do you admire Bobby, seeing him through Rory's eyes?

6. Are you conflicted, in your view of Bobby?
   Fully explain your point of view.

## General Vision and Viewpoint

Rory appears to be an optimistic character, looking forward to getting work with Bobby. His parents say that people like Bobby Mahon will put an end to the downturn, despite their circumstances they are hopeful and forward-looking.

Rory suffers from poor self-esteem. When he meets a girl, what should be something positive serves to sadden and frustrate him. He panics at the idea that this interaction might be the high point of his life, showing fear that he is doomed to failure. Despite having the girl's number, he decides not to go to the gig. He is afraid he will look stupid, and won't have the money to pay his way, imagining it all ending in shame and embarrassment, and so decides not to see her. He knows he will not pursue this relationship, and torments himself by going over it and thinking about the frustration he will feel.

It is sad that Rory chooses his empty life, feeling he is not capable of doing any better. His outlook is bleak and unhappy.

1. Is Rory an optimistic character?
   How does this affect the story's outlook?

2. Rory ends up wishing he never mentioned the possibility of working with Bobby to his parents.
   Why is this the case?
   How does this make you feel?

3. How does Rory feel about emigrating?
   Why is he considering moving to London?
   Do you feel sorry for him here?

4. How do people feel about the economy and the state of the country?
   How does this affect the atmosphere of the novel?

5. Is meeting the random girl at the gig poster a positive experience for Rory?
   Why won't he go to the gig?
   What insight does this give you into Rory's life?
   How does this part make you feel?

6. What is the mood like as the chapter ends?
   How do you feel at this point in the story?

7. How does Rory feel about himself?
   How does this impact on the general vision and viewpoint?

# Relationships

Rory spends a lot of time with Bobby. He refutes the idea that Bobby was having an affair, saying that Bobby is not interested in anyone other than his wife.

Rory wonders whether Bobby murdered his father as the circumstances surrounding finding the body suggest guilt. He wonders if Bobby had had enough of his dad, viewing him as a vicious old man. The bitter, destructive nature of their relationship was clearly easily seen. Rory gives the impression that Bobby's actions are understandable, given his awful relationship with his father.

Rory is considering giving up the idea of emigrating as his parents are so upset by the thought of him leaving. He feels he could not leave them distressed, showing that he cares about them.

1. Rory wonders why he told his parents about the possibility of working with Bobby.
   What does this section tell you about his relationships with his parents?

2. What stopped Rory from contacting Bobby since he got out on bail?
   What does this tell you about their relationship?

3. What motive does Rory suggest for Bobby murdering his father?
   What does this add to your understanding of their relationship?

4. What is preventing Rory from moving to London?
   What does this add to the theme of relationships?

5. Does Rory have a good relationship with Bobby Mahon? Support your view with examples from the text.

6. Why doesn't Rory ask his father to loan him some money?
What does this tell you about their relationship?

## Hero, Heroine, Villain

Rory's parents are delighted to hear that he might get work with Bobby. They say he is the sort of person to turn things around and get something up and running. They respect and admire Bobby, showing that he is viewed very positively in his community.

Rory dismisses the idea of Bobby having an affair with Réaltín, seeing him as completely faithful to his wife Triona.

Rory views Bobby as someone that people believe in. Rory sees it as a mix of imagination, confidence, and another unnamed quality. He sees Bobby as a leader, not someone who should be taking orders from someone else.

1. What opinion do Rory's parents have of Bobby?

2. Does Rory think that Bobby had an affair with Réaltín?

3. Does Rory think that Bobby murdered his father?

4. Does Rory admire Bobby?
What makes him feel this way about him?

5. According to Rory, how did Pokey Burke feel about Bobby?

# Chapter 16
# Millicent

Millicent talks about her parents arguing and the Children Snatcher Monster.

## Cultural Context/Social Setting

Millicent's father, Hughie, is out of work. Her mother works in Tesco and resents the financial strain the household is under due to Hughie's unemployment.

The account of the Children Snatcher Monster suggests that this world can be an unpredictable, frightening and dangerous place. Millicent's parents are fearful and worried to hear of a child's kidnapping. They are also helpless to do anything about it, as seen in Millicent's mother's frustrated attack on Hughie's competence as a father. The kidnapper is a threatening and very real presence in their world.

Millicent gets a terrible fright to see her father cry, because daddies never cry. Her words here sum up the pressure on men in this world to never express themselves emotionally. Hughie's breakdown is shocking and startling, because it is unheard of in this society for a man to cry.

1. What is a source of conflict and strain between Millicent's parents?
   What does this tell you about this world?

2. Hughie does not help a man with a metal leg when he sees him fall.
   What insight do his actions here give you into this world?

3. What is your impression of Millicent's mother's job? Does she like working in Tesco, do you think?

4. What does the story of the "Children Snatcher Monster" tell you about this world?

5. "...Daddy started *crying*, and I got an awful worser fright than when Mammy had started crying because daddies *never* cry..."
What insight do Millicent's words give you into this world?

6. What does Millicent's prayer at the end tell you about this world?

## Literary Genre

Millicent's chapter is told from a child's perspective. She is Lily's grandchild, her account demonstrates how the characters' stories overlap and interweave, adding depth to the reader's understanding of their lives and world.

Her account brings the kidnapping storyline into sharp focus, and makes clear how terrifying it is for a child to be taken like this. Her fear, and the concerns of her parents, are emotionally engaging, and provide an insight into how the community feels at this time.

1. What do you notice about this account?
Why has the author chosen this perspective?
What storyline does this perspective bring to mind?

2. Hughie is Millicent's father.
   How is he already connected to the narrative?
   What is the effect of this weaving of stories?

3. Is Millicent a perceptive child?
   What does this add to the story?

4. Is this an emotional account?
   Is it similar to or different from the other chapters in this regard?
   Use examples to support your ideas.

5. What does the "Children Snatcher Monster" add to the story?
   Be specific in your answer.

6. Comment on the image of Hughie crying with Millicent and her mother.
   What does this scene add to the story?

# General Vision and Viewpoint

Millicent's parents' arguments show their home is a very unhappy place. Millicent speaks of the "Children Snatcher Monster" taking a child, and how upset this made her mother, who then accused Hughie of not minding Millicent properly. Her mother's fear and helplessness is clear, as is her frustration when she takes it out on Hughie.

The threat of Millicent being taken fills her parents with fear and dread.

It is saddening that Millicent's mother attacks Hughie and accuses him of being incompetent. However, his tears act as a catalyst that brings about warmth and compassion in Millicent's mother. Her parents' fears are shared, they are united in their love for their daughter, which is a more hopeful, redeeming feature in the outlook here.

1. How does reading Millicent's description of her parents arguing make you feel?

2. Hughie does not help a man with a metal leg.
   What does this tell you about people, and life?

3. "I get really sad and I start crying before I know I'm going to."
   How does reading Millicent's account make you feel?
   How does it affect the general vision and viewpoint?

4. How do Millicent's parents react when they hear about the "Children Snatcher Monster"?

5. How does reading about Hughie crying make you feel?

6. Why can't Millicent sleep?
   Is there a sense of threat here?

7. How do you feel as the chapter ends?
   What details make you feel this way?

## Relationships

Millicent talks about her parents' arguments and her mother's scorn over her father's inability to earn a wage. This is a source of conflict in their home.
   While they argue a lot, her parents show real concern for Millicent.

When she is upset, arguments cease, and they direct their attention to her.

Millicent is aware of how unhappy her father is around her mother. She does not use bad language around her mother, as she does not want her father to get in trouble. This shows that Millicent realises he is a target for her mother's anger.

Millicent's mother reacts to news of the kidnapping by attacking Hughie for not minding Millicent well enough. He gets very upset, prompting a warmer response from her, where she rubs his arm and holds his hand. Their relationship is full of conflict, but it is not without compassion and love.

1. What are your impressions of Millicent's parents' relationship?
   What are the sources of conflict in their home?

2. Are Millicent's parents good parents?
   Use examples to support your view.

3. Is Millicent protective of her father?
   What does this suggest about her parents' relationship?

4. Why doesn't Millicent call her parents when she is afraid of the dark?
   What does this tell you about her relationship with them, and their relationship with each other?

## Hero, Heroine, Villain

Bobby Mahon is not mentioned in this chapter.

# Chapter 17
# Denis

Denis talks about the problems he is facing and the rage he feels. He reveals that he has killed Frank Mahon.

## Cultural Context/Social Setting

Denis has severe financial problems. He is owed almost a hundred grand, but cannot collect the money to pay his debts. As his chapter opens he cannot get out of bed. He mentions a man who killed himself because of financial difficulties. Denis' contribution makes clear the stress and panic suffered by those in financial distress in this world.

Denis' violent tendencies, and his killing of Frank Mahon, make clear the violence and anger of this world.

1. What is Denis' financial situation? How does this add to your understanding of the time and place of the story?

2. "Then it all went wallop and he done away with himself." What does this make you realise about the world of the novel?

3. What does Frank Mahon's murder reveal to you about this world?

## Literary Genre

Denis describes his financial situation as being very serious. He clearly details his building frustration as he is avoided by those who owe him money. He says he came very close to reacting violently in these situations. His anger and frustration give a sense of violence and conflict to come.

Annoyed about people giving out about the state of things, Denis states that he killed a man. This is a crucial development in the story. His admission here is exciting, as his confession means that Bobby is innocent. Our faith in Bobby, if waivering, is restored. That inner belief that Bobby did not commit such an act is proven correct, which is satisfying and involving for a reader. With Denis' revelation, there is hope of the positive resolution of the murder plotline.

There is a sense of desperation in Denis' actions as he describes the build-up to Frank's murder. Frank goaded him, and Denis responded by striking him in the head with a length of timber. Frank's vicious character is clear, even as he is murdered.

The chapter ends as it began, with Denis lying curled up in bed.

There is a sense of loss and frustration in this chapter, captured in Frank Mahon's senseless murder.

1. What state is Denis in as the chapter opens?
   What is the effect of this on the reader?

2. "Things was building up a long time inside in me."
   Does Denis' description of being avoided add tension here?
   Does it add a sense of foreboding or expectation?

3. How does Denis break the news that he killed a man to us?

What does this tell you about him?
What does this admission mean?

4. How did Frank Mahon react to an intruder in his home?
What does this reveal to you about him?

5. Is Denis an evil character?
How is he presented?
Fully explain your point of view.

6. Is the description of the murder believeable and realistic?

7. Is this an exciting chapter?
Give reasons for your answer.

8. Is this chapter important in terms of the overall story?
Explain your view.

9. Is this chapter a high point in the story?
Explain your point of view.

10. Is this chapter compelling to read?
Give reasons for your answer.

# General Vision and Viewpoint

Denis feels as though his world is falling in on him. Kate is barely tolerating him and he cannot get out of bed. He is facing major financial problems, and although he is owed almost a hundred grand, he is unlikely to get the money back. His situation is extremely bleak.

Denis' killing of Frank Mahon is a crime borne of rage and frustration.

It is a dark comment on the actions of people driven to desperation. In killing Frank, Denis imagines he is murdering his own father, a very dark action, resulting from a destructive, dysfunctional relationship. Denis' actions suggest a violent outlet for rage, frustration and suffering, a dark and saddening comment on life.

On a more positive note, Denis' guilt means that Bobby is innocent of this crime. Our faith in humanity is restored to some extent. Bobby's innocence suggests that good people do exist, our belief in him is no longer compromised.

1. "The sky is falling down."
   What sort of situation is Denis in?
   How does he feel about it?

2. Does Denis have someone he can turn to for help?
   What does this suggest about life?

3. What sort of person is Denis?
   What does he reveal about people and their actions?

4. Comment on Denis' motivation for speaking to Frank Mahon, and what it reveals about human nature.

5. Is there a sense of frustration and waste in this chapter?
   How does this affect the general vision and viewpoint?

6. Why did Denis kill Frank Mahon?
   How does this make you feel?

7. Denis has not been charged with Frank Mahon's murder.
   How does this make you feel?
   What does this suggest about life?

8. Does Denis' chapter bring darkness or light to the story? Fully explain your point of view.

## Relationships

This chapter is a very negative comment on the theme of relationships. Denis lacks a loving, supportive relationship, his interactions are marked by stress, frustration and rage.

He considers hitting his wife and driving over a man, and tears the wipers off the car of another man who refuses to talk to him about money he is owed. Denis cannot communicate how he feels in non-violent terms. His rage builds, until it finally finds violent release in the killing of Frank Mahon.

As he kills Frank, Denis imagines that he is killing his own father. This violent outburst is an act of hatred against his father, showing the destructive power of damaging relationships.

1. Describe Denis and Kate's relationship, as you see it.

2. What does Denis think, as he kills Frank Mahon? What insight does this give you into Denis' relationships?

3. What does this chapter contribute to the theme of relationships?

## Hero, Heroine, Villain

Denis' admission of committing murder means that Bobby is an innocent man. All of the rumours and talk about him are untrue. This chapter restores our faith in Bobby, as he has not killed his father. It also engages the reader's sympathy for Bobby as he is wrongly accused of this crime.

1. How does Denis feel about Bobby Mahon?
   What makes him feel this way?

2. Is Denis the story's villain?
   Fully explain your point of view.

3. Is Frank the story's villain?
   Fully explain your point of view.

4. How does this chapter affect your view of Bobby?
   Fully explain your point of view.

# Chapter 18
# Mags

Mags' father treats her coldly because she is gay, something he finds difficult to accept.

## Cultural Context/Social Setting

Mags, speaking of the kidnapping, says it does not seem natural for a young man to be a Montessori teacher. Her prejudice reveals the attitude that men are not capable of, and should not be interested in, caring roles or looking after young children.

Mags' father cannot accept her as a lesbian. Mags describes him as drowning in prejudice, he is unable to love her as he once did.

Mags mentions a change in the law that would give her and Ger the same legal standing as a heterosexual couple. This points towards a progressive, changing society on a larger scale, although prejudice is still present, as with her own father.

1. What does Mags' mother's attitude to blow-ins tell you about this place?

2. "It doesn't seem natural for a young *man* to be a Montessori teacher."
   What does Mags' prejudice reveal?

3. What does Mags' father's attitude to her being a lesbian reveal about this world?

4.     "That's just the way he was reared, Ger reckons."
How does Ger explain how Josie treats Mags?
What insight does this give you into the attitudes and behaviours of people in this world?

## Literary Genre

Mags talks about her father feeding his fat chickens. We know from an earlier chapter that this means her father is Josie. The story overlaps once more, showing how closely connected these characters are.

Mags' difficult relationship with her father is similar to other difficult, flawed relationships in the text. This is a prominent theme, showing the heartache that results from negative relationships.

1. How does Mags fit into the story?

2. Does Mags' relationship with her father mirror or echo any other relationships in the text?
What point is the author making here?

3. What themes or strands of the story does Mags' chapter add to and support?

## General Vision and Viewpoint

Mags knows there is a gulf between her and her father. He does not accept her because she is a lesbian. It is saddening and disheartening that he cannot accept her for who she is.

Her father lets her down, showing that sometimes loved ones do not live up to being the people we need them to be, a saddening comment on human relationships.

1. "The way he talks to Eamonn and my niece and nephew."
   What does Mags realise about her father?
   How does this make you feel?

2. How does Mags mentioning the kidnapping affect the mood?
   Are you hopeful about Dylan's safety?

3. How does Mags' recollection of the dinner party make you feel?
   What does her father's lack of understanding and acceptance reveal about life?

4. Does this chapter end on a sad or hopeful note?
   Explain your point of view.

5. Does this chapter give you the sense that sometimes those we love and need most let us down?
   Explain your point of view with reference to the text.

## Relationships

Mags knows that her father does not want to talk to her. He cannot accept that she is a lesbian. His prejudice has changed how he acts towards her, and how he feels about her. Mags realises this, and wishes he remembered how he loved her. Their relationship is damaged and marked by distance, and Mags wishes it were different.

Their relationship lacks love, warmth and understanding, and so is very similar to other relationships in the novel.

1. What is lacking in Mags' relationship with her father?

2. What does the dinner party recollection reveal about Mags' relationship with her father?

3. What insight does Ger provide into how parents react when a child is in danger?
   Is there truth in her words, in the context of the novel? Explain your point of view.

4. How does Mags feel about her father?

5. What does this chapter add to the theme of relationships? Use examples to support your view.

## Hero, Heroine, Villain

Bobby Mahon is not mentioned in this chapter.

# Chapter 19
# Jim

Jim, the local garda sergeant, talks about the kidnapping, Frank Mahon's murder, and crime and violence.

## Cultural Context/Social Setting

The old woman who visits the garda station focuses on crime in this world. She mentions kidnapping, murder and rape, showing how dangerous and violent a place this can be.

Jim mentions his nephew's drowning, tying his story to Bridie's. Their world is a shared place, full of common ground. Through Jim's reference he reminds us that this is a place of loss and sadness.

Jim ends his account by speaking of violent and tragic events in the community, ending with thoughts on violent events from the war against the British. This creates the impression that violence, tragedy and opposition are part of this world, constantly resurfacing and repeating over time. This place is steeped in sadness, violence and tragedy.

1. What does the account of the old woman in the garda station tell you about this world?

2. Does Jim share the old woman's views? What does this suggest?

3. What insight into the media does Jim provide? How do they contribute to this world?

4. Is Jim a religious character?
   Give reasons for your answer.

5. What gives Réaltín a solid link to this place?
   What does this tell you about people in this world and their attitude to place and belonging?

6. "Them armed response lads blew that poor boy to Kingdom Come…"
   How does Jim's account of what happened to the Cunliffe boy add to your understanding of this world?

7. What events does Jim talk about as this chapter ends?
   How does this add to your sense of this place?

## Literary Genre

The grim reality of Dylan's disappearance is made clear in this account. Jim has access to all of the available information, and has no idea where the boy is. His worry and apprehension create tension and a sense of foreboding in this chapter, due to his first person perspective.

His description of Seanie Shaper's upset adds an emotional charge to this account. The sense of fear and hopelessness builds and can be felt by the reader.

Jim describes finding Bobby standing over his dead father. When asked if he did it, Bobby replied that he did not know. Bobby's failure to clear his name adds tension to this strand of the story. However, as we know that Denis committed this murder, it is also frustrating that Bobby does not protest his innocence.

Timmy supplies Jim with accurate information about the kidnapping.

Jim is very suspicious of the Montessori teacher, which is tense, exciting and involving for the reader, who wishes Jim would act on his suspicions.

1. This chapter begins in the garda station.
   What does this add to the story?

2. Comment on the imagery as Jim lies awake.
   What does it add to the story?

3. Jim remembers his nephew's drowning and describes his helplessness and loss.
   What does this recollection, at this point, add to Jim's account?
   How does it impact on the reader?

4. How does Jim's description of how distraught Seanie Shaper is add to the story here?

5. What does the account of finding Bobby by his dead father add to the story?
   Is this tense or frustrating?
   Explain your point of view.

6. What made Timmy visit the garda station?
   Is this an exciting development?

7. How does Jim react to Timmy's information?
   Does this increase reader tension and anticipation?
   Fully explain your point of view.

8. "But that Montessori teacher is awful suspicious if you ask me."

Is this a tense point in the story?
What do you want to happen next?

## General Vision and Viewpoint

The old woman in the police station deplores the violence of the world around her. She speaks of kidnapping, murder and rape, and their prevalence in the world. Her fear, and this ever present violence, darkens the outlook and creates the impression that the world is a vicious, violent place, full of darkness and uncontrolled chaos.

Jim cannot sleep. He lies in the dark, wondering where the boy could be. He thinks of his nephew, drowned years ago. Jim's outlook is dark and bleak, he is deeply upset by the kidnapping. His emotion, and sense of grief here, contributes to a bleak general vision and viewpoint.

Despite Bobby's failure to protest his innocence, Jim does not believe that he killed his father. Jim's faith in Bobby brightens the outlook here, as it suggests faith in people and a refusal to jump to negative conclusions. This is a glimmer of hope and positivity, in an otherwise bleak and harrowing chapter.

Overall, there is a great sense of loss and regret in Jim's account, as he speaks of his nephew's drowning, Frank Mahon's murder, the kidnapping, and the shooting of the Cunliffe boy. This creates a sense of needless loss of life and sadness, showing life to be full of violence and sorrow.

1. What do the old woman's words as the chapter begins reveal about her outlook?
   How does this affect the general vision and viewpoint?

2. What does the old woman suggest she will do because of the state of the country?
How does this affect the general vision and viewpoint?

3. "All I think about is that little boy, and where in the name of God he could be."
Describe Jim's outlook here.
How does this contribute to the general vision and viewpoint?

4. Jim feels responsible for the death of his nephew.
How does this affect the general vision and viewpoint?

5. Does Jim believe that Bobby is a murderer?
How does this affect the outlook in this chapter?

6. Generally, how does Jim feel about members of his community?
Does this create a positive or negative impression in this chapter?

7. "But that Montessori teacher is awful suspicious if you ask me."
How do characters like Trevor and Lloyd impact on the general vision and viewpoint?

8. Do you think there is any hope of finding Dylan?
Explain your point of view.

9. Is there a sense of regret in this chapter?
Use examples to support your view.

10. Does Jim create the sense that life is troubled and violent in his account?
Include examples in your answer.

11. Where do you see reasons to be hopeful in this chapter? Fully explain your point of view.

## Relationships

Jim mentions violent and upsetting events that have taken place. As a garda, he must deal with these violent and upsetting events, and so has had many negative and saddening interactions.

1. What sort of relationship does Jim have with members of the public?

2. How does Jim view Bobby Mahon?

3. What does Jim's insight into the murder case add to your understanding of Bobby's relationship with his father?

4. Does Jim's account depict relationships positively or negatively?
What characterises the relationships Jim encounters? Include examples to support your point of view.

## Hero, Heroine, Villain

Jim gives an insight into Bobby's actions at the time of his father's death. Jim says Bobby phoned him to come to his father's house where Frank Mahon lay dead. Calling the police is the responsible thing to do here, and it is not surprising that Bobby does so. However, when asked if he committed the crime, Bobby says that he does not know. This shows how shocked Bobby is, but also how much he doubts himself. We know from Denis' account that Bobby did not murder his father, but Bobby is not sure of his own innocence. Perhaps, because he hated him so much, Bobby cannot believe that he did not kill him.

1. What does Jim's account of finding Bobby with his dead father add to your understanding of Bobby's character?

2. Bobby phoned the police to report finding his father's body.
   Does this surprise you?

3. "When I asked him was it he did it, he told me he didn't know."
   What is your response to this?

4. Does Jim think Bobby is the murderer?
   What makes him think this way?

5. What does this chapter add to your understanding of Bobby as a person?

# Chapter 20
# Frank

Frank's ghostly account gives an insight into his relationships with his wife, son and his abusive father.

## Cultural Context/Social Setting

Frank lives in the cottage he was born in, as did his father before him, and so is tied to the land he has neglected.

Frank recounts his father viciously beating him when he did well in school, showing the violence of this world, and an intolerance for what is seen as pride. It shows this world to be a harsh place, where love and warmth are absent, and men behave violently. Although he was a child, his father beat him severely with a pipe length, and left him where he fell. This sums up the toxic masculinity of this world, where explosive anger dominates and violence is a means of communication.

It is worth noting that this violence and viciousness continues through the generations, in Frank's case it was his sharp tongue that caused pain to his family. This is a world where characters are quick to hurt one another, and slow to speak of understanding.

Frank's account adds to the idea that this world is a closed, unfeeling, violent place.

1. "The Vatican done away with Purgatory, I'd say that's why I'm being left here to haunt my own house."
   What do Frank's thoughts reveal about his beliefs?

2. Frank lived his whole life in this cottage, like his father before him.
What does this add to your understanding of this place?

3. How did Frank treat his wife and son?
What impression does this give you of this world?

4. How was Frank treated by his father?
What does this tell you about this world?

5. Frank wonders how he treated Bobby as he did, considering his own hatred of his father.
Do Frank's actions and behaviour surprise you, considering the world he lived in?
Fully explain your point of view.

## Literary Genre

Frank's point of view in this chapter adds a unique perspective to the narrative, as he gives his account as some sort of ghost. It is satisfying to hear Frank's account, as we have read so much about him and view him as a figure who is universally disliked. Reading his chapter allows us to understand what made him the man that he became and feel some pity for him.

Frank's chapter provides insight into his difficult, destructive relationship with Bobby. He knows that he has mistreated Bobby and Bobby's mother, cutting them with his words.

This chapter adds to the theme of relationships, and more specifically, to the idea of fathers having poor relationships with their sons. Frank's father was angry and violent, Frank himself was vicious and cutting. Both Frank and Bobby imagined killing their fathers, as Denis did when he murdered Frank. There is a simmering hatred directed towards hateful fathers that comes to the fore in this chapter.

1. What are your impressions of Frank, from reading this chapter?

2. What does Frank speaking about his father add to the story?

3. "...I'd picture myself with my two hands around my father's throat..."
Is this a recurring image in the novel?
What is the author suggesting here?
What does this image add to the storytelling?

4. Were you expecting a chapter from Frank?
What does his perspective, at this point in the novel, add to the story?

5. Is this a very honest chapter?
In a way, has the story been building towards Frank's account?
Explain your point of view.

6. Is Frank a likeable character?
Does he have any redeeming qualities?

7. Do you enjoy the supernatural aspect of this chapter?
Give a reason for your answer.
What does this aspect add to the story?

8. What does Frank's chapter add to the story?

9. Is this a satisfying chapter from a reader's perspective? Fully explain your point of view.

## General Vision and Viewpoint

Frank speaks of having to bring balance to how Bobby was treated by his mother, and having to prepare him for life in the hard world. It seems his hard, cruel ways were supposed to have some benefit. It is saddening that Frank got this so wrong.

Frank feels his wife had a superiority complex and looked down on him. His bitterness and the anger he directed towards her portrays a very negative way of living.

Frank's account of being beaten by his father as a boy is upsetting and saddening. The violent aggression of his father shows how people can be hurt by those who should love and protect them, a negative comment on life. This destructive relationship has helped shape Frank's relationships in life, making him bitter and vicious. This gives a bleak view of life, where fathers treat their sons with such violence and contempt.

Frank speaks about imagining himself killing his father, and comments on the waste of it, to imagine himself so. The idea of waste and lost opportunity is especially marked now that Frank has been murdered by a stranger, another wasteful, senseless action. The idea of waste, and loss, adds to the outlook throughout the novel. Life is presented as trying and difficult, steeped in loss and the ghost of what might have been.

Frank wonders how he treated Bobby as he did, considering how much he hated his own father. There is a sense of a ravaging, destructive hatred here, destroying Frank and his relationships with others. This is a dark, bleak idea, adding to the novel's dark outlook. Life is portrayed as cruel and harrowing, with those that should love us, hurting us most.

1. "The future is a cold mistress."
   What does Frank mean here when he speaks of the future?

2. What sort of death had Frank imagined?

3. How does Frank view life?
   How did this impact on his relationship with Bobby?

4. How did Frank treat his wife?
   How does this make you feel?
   What made him treat her this way?
   How does this make you feel?

5. "I knew I was doing it and I couldn't stop. God help us, I could never stop at either of them."
   Frank was aware of how badly he treated Bobby and Bobby's mother, but felt helpless to change his behaviour.
   How does this make you feel?
   What sort of comment is this on life?

6. How did Frank react to seeing his grandchild?
   Why couldn't he express himself here?
   How does this make you feel?

7. Do you feel sorry for Frank when you read about his father beating him?
   What does this reveal to you about Frank's life?
   Did this beating affect his outlook, do you think?
   Fully explain your point of view.

8. Frank says he is not a violent man.
   Did he manage not to repeat his father's violent ways?
   Explain your point of view fully.

9. What used Frank imagine when he drank?
   How does this impact on the general vision and viewpoint?

10. "Imagine the waste of it, thinking about killing a dead man."
    Is there a sense of waste in this chapter?
    Is there a sense of waste throughout the novel?
    Fully explain your point of view.

11. Is this a very bleak, harrowing chapter?
    Are sections of it difficult to read?
    Explain your point of view.

12. What is the impact of negative relationships on the general vision and viewpoint here?
    Use examples to support the points that you make.

13. What is the tone like as the chapter ends?

14. How do you feel as the chapter ends?

15. How does this chapter impact on the novel's general vision and viewpoint?

## Relationships

Frank describes how vicious and hurtful he was towards his wife and son. He was aware of how he hurt them, but could not change his behaviour.

He describes how wonderful his wife thought Bobby was, and how he felt the need to counteract this loving, supportive relationship and tear it asunder.

Frank remembers a time when he went to his father expecting praise for doing well in school, and was beaten with a length of wavin pipe. The violence and hurt he suffered at his father's hands may help to explain his bitter, vicious nature, and the hurtful, destructive way he treated his wife and son. It is saddening to see how his relationship with others suffered as a result of his damaged relationship with his father.

The idea of hating one's father and wanting to kill them has appeared many times in the novel. It is not surprising that Frank also hated his father, just as his son hates him. Indeed, the man who killed Frank pictured himself killing his own father. This idea of destructive, hate-filled father-son relationships is emphasised here, showing the seriously damaging side of negative relationships.

1. Is Frank aware of how Bobby feels about him?

2. What is Frank's attitude towards Bobby not clearing his name?
   What insight does this give you into their relationship?

3. What sort of relationship did Frank and his wife have? How did he treat her?

4. How did Bobby's mother feel about Bobby, according to Frank?

5. How did Frank feel when he first saw his grandchild?
   What does this suggest?

6. Is Frank forever taking swipes at Bobby?
   Explain your point of view.

7. How was Frank treated by his father?
   Do you think this affected his relationship with Bobby?

8. How does Frank feel about the way he treated Bobby?

9. Does Frank care about his son?
   Fully explain your point of view.

## Hero, Heroine, Villain

It is clear from this chapter that Bobby's hatred of his father is justified. Frank speaks harshly about Bobby, calling him stupid and vain. He makes it clear that he has always been quick to put Bobby down and speak sharply to him. Where others admire Bobby, Frank fails to see his son's strengths.

Frank's account further cements Bobby's innocence, as he gives the details of his murder. We also see the impact of his father's death on Bobby. Although they had an awful relationship, Bobby does not appear to take any joy in his father's passing.

1. How does Frank speak about Bobby?

2. How did Frank treat his son?

3. What insight does Frank's chapter give you into Bobby's upbringing and character?

# Chapter 21
# Triona

Triona talks about her husband and how much she loves him. She mentions Bobby's difficulty in talking about upsetting things and his relationship with his father. She also tells us Dylan has been found alive and well.

## Cultural Context/Social Setting

Triona speaks of Bobby's good standing in the community and how he is looked up to.

She draws on details of their life, such as Bobby's involvement in GAA, and local gossip, to create the impression of a rural town where there is both a sense of togetherness and nosy judgement. She doubts the sincerity of the tight-knit community and questions whether people really were worried for the missing child, or were more caught up in their own problems.

When she speaks about Bobby's difficulty talking to her about things that upset him, she adds to the impression that this is a world where men find it hard to be openly emotional or vulnerable. Men are emotionally stifled, and find it hard to talk about their problems and sadness.

1. What does Auntie Bernadette show you about this place?

2. What does the conversation of the "herd of donkeys" reveal to you about the way men and women are viewed in this society?

3. What purpose does religion serve in Bernadette's life? How does this add to your impression of this world?

4. What does the club awards ceremony tell you about this place?
Do people have fun here?

5. "How many of them really cared about the little boy?"
What truths does Triona realise about the attitudes of some people in her community?

6. "When Frank was killed they must have nearly exploded with pleasure."
What is Triona suggesting about the locals here?

7. Jim Gildea rescues the boy, restoring order to this world.
What does this tell you about this place?

## Literary Genre

Triona, Bobby's wife, is the final speaker in the story, hers is the final word in the narrative. Her appreciation of Bobby's goodness, and her understanding of his character and his troubled relationship with his father emerges very clearly in this chapter, as does a sense of the place where the story is set.

Triona talks about Bobby's inability to open up to her, a lack of being able to express how he feels. This is characteristic of many of the relationships in the story, and appears to be a by-product of the society of the text. In this way, Triona's account reinforces some of the key ideas we have come across over the course of the novel.

She is open, honest and sincere in her chapter, just as the others were. The main difference is that Triona is hopeful and positive, ending the story with an emphasis on the importance of love, not hate.

She also completes the kidnapping strand, telling us that the boy has been recovered alive and well. This further adds to the positive ending, a great tragedy has been averted, disaster is never certain. The fact that each of the plot threads has been completed makes for a satisfying ending from a reader's perspective.

1. What does Triona's story about Bernadette and Coley make clear?

2. Explain the significance of the symbol of the spinning heart, according to Triona.

3. How does Triona add to your understanding of Bobby's character?
Be specific in your answer.

4. How does Triona depict Frank?
(Consider the language she uses when speaking about him).
How does this affect your view of him?

5. What does Triona add to your sense of the story's setting?

6. Dylan is found alive at the end of the story.
What does this bring to the story?
What do the details surrounding his rescue bring to the story?

7. Is this a triumphant ending?
Explain your view.

8. Why has the author chosen to complete the story with Triona's account?
   Why place her chapter here?

## General Vision and Viewpoint

Triona talks about the beginning of her relationship with Bobby. She describes him as someone set apart from the other men, with depth and sensitivity. The admiration she holds him in, and her understanding of him, are positive, gladdening details in this final chapter.

Triona is aware of the deep trauma and hurt Bobby has suffered because of his father. She has not pushed him to talk about it, she just lets him know that she knows he is in pain and will help him when he is ready. Her patience and understanding add positivity to this final chapter. Here is somebody caring and compassionate, willing to do what it takes to help Bobby feel better about himself and heal the hurt from years past.

Triona feels a sense of injustice that Frank Mahon lived, while her own lovely father became ill and died. She reminds us that life is not fair, or predictable, and that death is very much a part of life.

She doubts the sincerity of her community's concern over the child being snatched, believing that people are self-centred and selfish, consumed with their own problems rather than the plight of others, a bleak and disheartening thought.

Triona understands Bobby completely, and accepts him exactly as he is. This is a positive addition to the novel's message and outlook.

The recovery of Dylan at the end adds hope and optimism to the story's outlook. Freedom and happiness are possible.

This final chapter adds hope and positivity to what is a dark, troubled and pessimistic text overall.

1. How did Triona feel about Bobby when she first spoke to him?
   How does this make you feel?

2. What happened to Coley?
   How does this make you feel?

3. Did Triona think that Bobby was having an affair?
   How does this make you feel?

4. Is Triona afraid that Bobby is a murderer?
   What does this tell you about how she feels about Bobby?
   How does this make you feel?

5. "His putdowns put her in the ground."
   What is Triona suggesting here?
   Is this a bleak or saddening idea?

6. Has Triona helped Bobby with his private pain and suffering?
   Is she a positive, nurturing influence, in your view?
   Explain your stance fully.

7. What was life like, living with Frank?
   What sort of existence is this?
   How does this make you feel?

8. Was it difficult for Bobby to talk about living with Frank?
   How does this make you feel?

9. How does Triona feel towards Frank?
   How does this affect the general vision and viewpoint?

10. What does the story of Triona's father's illness add to the general vision and viewpoint?
    What comment does his illness make about life?

11. Triona doubts the sincerity of the concern the community felt when the child was taken.
    What sort of comment is this on people and their attitudes?
    How does this make you feel?

12. How does Triona feel towards the Teapot Taliban?
    What outlook do they have?
    How does this make you feel?

13. Dylan is recovered safe and well.
    How does this influence the general vision and viewpoint?
    Is Jim Gildea a hero?
    How does Dylan's safe recovery make you feel?

14. "What matters only love?"
    How does the novel's last line affect its outlook?
    Is this a hopeful ending?
    Explain your view.

15. Does the chapter end on a high or a low point?
    Give a reason for your answer.

16. How do you feel as the story ends?
    Give a reason for your answer.

# Relationships

Triona speaks about how Bobby is different to other men. She saw fear, doubt, shyness and sadness in him when she first spoke to him, and he became the only one she was interested in. There is a great sense of admiration and devotion when Triona speaks of Bobby here.

Triona never thought that Bobby was unfaithful, and would not love him any less if he had killed his father. This shows real belief and love on Triona's part.

What Triona struggles with is that Bobby would not talk to her while he was out on bail. His inability to communicate with her, and express himself emotionally, is the most significant flaw in their relationship.

1. What did Triona recognise in Bobby when she first met him?

2. "I was wrapped in him from that minute."
   Explain what Triona means here.
   What does this tell you about their relationship?

3. What comparison does Triona draw between Bernadette and Coley and Frank and Bobby?
   What does this add to the theme of relationships?

4. "Coley didn't survive Bernadette's terrible reign over his childhood."
   What is Triona suggesting here?
   What does this say about Coley's relationship with Bernadette?

5. Did Triona think that Bobby had been unfaithful? What does this tell you about their relationship and how she views her husband?

6. What did Triona struggle with when Bobby was out on bail?

7. "I don't even care if he *did* kill Frank. I wouldn't love him any less." What insight does this give you into how Triona feels about Bobby?

8. How does Triona sum up Bobby's relationship with his parents? Is she accurate here?

9. Does Triona know her husband well?

10. Triona suspects that Bobby spoke to her about growing up with Frank for her benefit. What does this suggest about how he feels about her?

11. What made Triona hate Frank at the club awards ceremony? What does this reveal about how Triona feels about Bobby? What does this reveal about Frank's relationship with his son?

12. Did Bobby have a good relationship with Triona's father?

13. Did Triona have a good relationship with her father?
    Does this bring balance to this theme, in your view?

14. Does Triona truly love and understand Bobby?
    What does this add to the theme of relationships?

15. Do Triona and Bobby have a loving, committed relationship in your opinion?
    Use examples to illustrate your ideas.

## Hero, Heroine, Villain

Triona sees all of the private pain and suffering in Bobby. She understands how he has been hurt by his father, is saddened by his mother's death, and how he feels he is a failure for not protecting his mother better from his father's cruel words.

Triona knows that people look up to Bobby. She mentions the club awards ceremony as a time when Bobby realised how much people thought of him.

He is a sensitive character, with hidden depths, who is admired and loved very much by his wife.

1. "He stood with but was never a part of the herd of donkeys."
   What is Triona saying about Bobby here?

2. What were Triona's first impressions of Bobby?
   Did she judge his character well?
   Explain your point of view.

3. Was Triona concerned that Bobby was having an affair with Réaltín?
What does this tell you about Bobby?

4. When Bobby was out on bail, he did not talk to Triona. Why, do you think, is this the case?

5. "Bobby hated his father and never got over his mother and thought of himself as a failure for not protecting her properly from his father's cruel tongue."
Is this an accurate picture of Bobby, in your view?
Give reasons for your answer.

6. Do people look up to Bobby Mahon?
What makes them feel this way about him?
Use examples to support the points that you make.

7. Does Bobby know how he affects people?
What does this tell you about him?

8. Do you think you would like Bobby Mahon, if you met him?
Give reasons for your point of view.

# The Comparative Study

# Cultural Context/Social Setting

*Cultural Context/Social Setting refers to the world of the text.
Consider social norms, beliefs, values and attitudes.*

'The Spinning Heart' takes place during the economic recession in Ireland, that took place from 2008. This economic context adds a lot to the setting, as it explains the lack of money, employment opportunity and hope at the time. The novel is centred around a fictitious Irish town. Although its exact location is not stated, it is somewhere in the midwest region.

A striking feature of the society in the novel is the toxic masculinity that is evident. Men are incapable of expressing how they feel, or acknowledging emotional upset or weakness. Bobby Mahon is unable to speak freely with his wife about what upsets him most, while Seanie Shaper keeps his struggle with depression hidden.

Another aspect of the way men behave in this society is the anger and violence that many of them demonstrate. Frank Mahon speaks of his father beating him, and reveals the vicious, cutting way he treated his wife and son. Denis is an explosive character, erupting into a violent rage on a number of occasions, before beating Frank Mahon to death. In this world, men express themselves through physical anger.

Lloyd and Trevor plotting and kidnapping Dylan adds to this picture of destructive, dangerous men. Their actions show this world to be a menacing, threatening place, where children are not safe and laws are not obeyed.

Women are viewed as sexual objects by many of the male characters, they are described in terms of sex and their bodies. Few men appear to have an emotional connection to or understanding of women. Lily details being viciously beaten when Bernie discovered that she had revealed him as her baby's father. The contempt and violence she is treated with here shows how little she matters to Bernie. The fact that she is a prostitute further alienates her. Bernie never considered himself to be in a relationship with Lily, failing to see beyond her label of sex worker.

The world of the novel seems like a sad place. Each chapter gives an account of the private sufferings and sorrow of each character. They suffer from grief and loss, from feeling misunderstood and unloved, and fail to share these problems and inadequacies with others. This makes this world a lonely place, where characters struggle and suffer alone, unable to ask for help or discuss their problems.

There is a lack of hope in this world, as jobs are hard to come by. The spectre of emigration hangs over many families, who would prefer if their sons did not have to move abroad to work.

Family is something that is prioritised in this world. Brian does not want to emigrate as it will upset his parents, Réaltín speaks of her bond with her father. Even Bobby, who despises his father, visits him daily, showing how important family is in this world.

A sense of belonging to this place is also prized in this community. Frank speaks of living his whole life in the same cottage that his father lived in, Timmy's nana similarly lived her whole life a small distance from where she was born. Réaltín is viewed as a blow-in until it is learned that Seanie Shaper is her son's father, then attitudes to her change, and she is felt to belong to the community.

This emphasis on belonging to this place goes hand in hand however with local gossip, rumours and speculation. Characters spitefully discuss the misfortunes of others, jumping to conclusions and relaying all the gory, often invented, details. There is much talk of Bobby killing his father and having an affair with Réaltín, although neither are true. In this small town, everything is up for comment and discussion.

Overall, this is a distressed, dejected place, suffering badly due to financial collapse, where men cannot speak about their feelings and act violently, to devastating consequences.

1. Briefly describe the setting of the novel.
   Consider when and where it is set.

2. What is the role of women in the world of the novel?
   How do men view women in this world?
   (Consider the language used to speak about women, and how women are treated.)

3. What is the role of men in the world of the novel?
   What expectations are there on men in this world?
   Do men struggle with the expectations placed on them?

4. What holds men back from pursuing relationships in this text?
   What does this tell you about this world?

5. How are children treated in the world of the novel?

6. How are workers treated in this novel?
   What does this reveal about the attitudes of those in authority/power?

7. Is this a fun place for the novel's characters' to live?
   Are there opportunities for these characters in this world?
   Explain your point of view.

8. Does the world of 'The Spinning Heart' make it easy or difficult for characters to be happy?
   Use examples to support your ideas.

9. Is the world of the novel a difficult place for Bobby to negotiate?
Give reasons for your answer.

10. If the cultural context/social setting were different, would Bobby's relationship with his wife, Triona, be easier?
Use examples to support the points that you make.

11. If the cultural context/social setting were different, would Bobby's relationship with his father, Frank, be easier?
Use examples to support the points that you make.

12. Bobby cannot express himself properly to his wife, Triona.
To what extent is this due to the cultural context/social setting?

13. Is the world of the novel traditional and rigid or relaxed?
Give reasons for your answer.

14. Is marriage significant in this world?
Use examples to support your point of view.

15. Are money, wealth and property important in this world?
Is school and academia important in this world?
What is valued in the world of this novel?
What does this tell you about this place?

16. What are the biggest problems facing characters in this world?

17. What attitudes do you notice most in this society?

18. Is there a lot of private, personal suffering in the world of the novel?
Why is this the case?
How does the cultural context/social setting contribute to this suffering?

19. By all accounts, Bobby's mother had a terrible life with Frank.
Based on your understanding of the social setting/cultural context, why, do you think, did she stay with him?
Use examples to support your views and opinions.

20. Are you shocked by the violence of the world of the novel?
Explain your point of view.

21. What is considered to be unacceptable behaviour in this world?
Include examples to support your view.
Are you surprised, shocked or saddened to encounter some of the 'acceptable behaviour' in this world?
Fully explain your point of view, including examples.

22. Who is the violence directed towards in this world?
What does this suggest about this society?

23. Is this a caring or cruel society?
Support your answer with reference to the text.

24. Is religion important to characters in this world?
Use examples to support your point of view.

# Literary Genre

*Literary Genre refers to the way the story is told. Consider aspects of narration such as the manner and style of narration, characterisation, setting, tension, literary techniques, etc.*

## Structure

It is worth considering the novel format itself when considering the novel's structure. Reading is a solitary activity, even when a group is read to aloud, the action occurs in each reader's imagination. This can be a very absorbing, immersive method of storytelling, as each reader pictures events unfolding from within the author's world of words.

This novel is made up of twenty-one honest, deeply personal and confessional accounts. Characters reveal their failings and shortcomings, and the saddest details of their lives. Due to the honesty and sincerity of each account, this is a very appealing stylistic feature. Also, as the characters all know each other and live in the same world, our overall impression of the story and this place is gradually added to and built up over the course of the novel as stories overlap and intertwine.

The novel's structure adds to tension and reader anticipation also. When an exciting event occurs, we wait to learn more about the event from another speaker. This makes the narrative involving and engaging for readers. Also, as readers, we have to decide who to believe and what to disbelieve, another exciting aspect of this structured approach. In particular, it is interesting to see how our view of Bobby Mahon is tested over the course of the novel. As the novel's protagonist, he begins the narrative, and each subsequent chapter adds to our view of and understanding of him, this place and these characters' lives.

When characters suggest that Bobby has been unfaithful, or that he has committed murder, it is difficult not to be swayed by them, and remain convinced of Bobby's innocence. This is a very involving feature of the narrative, it is as if the reader themselves is a member of this community, judging Bobby on rumour and hearsay, while simultaneously hoping he is the good man we believe him to be.

## Character

Bobby is completely honest and truthful in the novel's first chapter, revealing intimate details of his life, such as his hatred of his father, his love for his wife, and the deep loss and grief he bears following his mother's death. His vulnerability makes him very likeable and relatable, and it is easy to be drawn into his life story. He emerges as a sensitive character, who cannot discuss his emotions and upset with his wife. His murderous feelings towards his father make him feel real and human, reading of his upbringing, it is esay to understand why he feels this way about his father. As readers, we feel for Bobby, empathising with his struggles and sorrows.

The following chapters add to the reader's sense of Bobby's character; he is handsome, sound and universally admired in his community. The positive regard he is held in reinforces the reader's sense that Bobby is a good man.

Our sense of Bobby's character is tested by the rumours of him having an affair, and by his presence when his father's murdered body is discovered. These doubts are put to rest by further testimonies that follow. Rory in particular, rubbishes the idea of Bobby being unfaithful, while Denis admits to the murder in his chapter. In this way, our faith in Bobby is restored, in fact, the reader may even be pleased and relieved to discover his innocence, such is the connection with this troubled, sensitive lead character.

## Tension

Much of the novel's tension revolves around Bobby's destructive relationship with his father. This flawed relationship is full of hatred, spite and bad feeling, and so captures the reader's imagination, making us want to know more. It is therefore a very exciting, climactic moment, when we learn that Frank Mahon has been murdered, perhaps by his own son, and the wait to discover the truth is agonising.

Similarly, the kidnapping storyline offers the tense threat of violence, and perhaps even murder, and so is very emotionally involving for the reader. Trevor, the instigator of the kidnapping, is deluded, entertaining fantasies of killing his mother and her friend for being witches, and enjoying a romance with Réaltín, the kidnapped boy's mother. He is a dangerous, unpredictable character, and his plans and the kidnapping itself add drama and suspense to the storyline.

Indeed, the rumours of Bobby and Réaltín's supposed affair add tension, as they make us question what we know of Bobby and suggest conflict to come.

The novel's structure lends itself well to creating and sustaining tension, as once a chapter ends, the reader must wait for the next speaker to add to a particularly interesting or exciting thread of action. This adds to the novel's tension, encouraging the reader to keep reading, to discover what will happen next.

## Conflict

This is a conflict rich text, with many accounts featuring physical violence, or the threat of violence to come, as with Lily's account of being beaten, or Denis' account of his explosive anger and Frank Mahon's murder.

The murder storyline and Bobby's alleged guilt adds conflict, as does the kidnapping storyline and the threat to the community it represents.

Local rumours also create conflict with the suggestion that Bobby has been unfaithful. This further shakes our faith in him, and suggests that there may be more problems to come.

Ryan's use of conflict and his inclusion of threatening and violent characters adds to the excitement of the text, making the reader want to read on to uncover exciting action and see what happens next.

The image of killing one's horrible father is one that is returned to frequently throughout the text, keeping conflict and negative family relationships to the fore of the story.

## Imagery and Symbolism

The world of the story is described very beautifully, giving a very clear sense of place to the novel.

The idea of drowning occurs a couple of times, first with Bridie's account of her young son's death, and again when Seanie Shaper contemplates suicide and speaks of local women drowning in a lake. The author uses natural imagery to depict these sad deaths, creating a sense of loss, grief and sadness in the novel. In this way, the imagery is evocative and atmospheric, adding to the mood of the story.

Réaltín's ghost estate could be considered to be a symbol for the financial collapse and ruin that contributes so much to the setting. Her lonely life in a ruined estate is a poignant reminder of the country's economic collapse.

## The Vernacular/Demotic

The novel is rich in the language of real, ordinary Irish people, which adds to the authenticity of each speaker's chapter. The rhythms of language and expressions used are entirely real and accurate, lending the sense of spoken accounts to the text. This adds to the confessional feel of each chapter, as each speaker opens up and reveals their darkest fears and feelings, and truest selves.

1. How is this story told? (Consider the novel format)
   Why is the story told in this way?
   What is the effect of this?

2. How does the novel's opening arouse your interest and curiosity?

3. What are your first impressions of Bobby?
   Does your view of him change as you read on?
   Explain your point of view.

4. Where and when does this story take place?
   Be specific in your answer.

5. How important is the murder storyline in the novel?
   Is it simply a plot device to introduce conflict, or does it bring more to the story?
   Is the murder storyline involving and engaging?
   Include examples to support your view.

6. Did you expect or anticipate Frank Mahon's murder?
   What does this add to the storytelling?

7. How significant a plot point is Denis' account of Frank's death?
   Explain your point of view.

8. How important is the kidnapping storyline in the novel?
   Is it simply a plot device to introduce conflict, or does it bring more to the story?
   Include examples to support your view.

9. Does Donal Ryan foreshadow the child's kidnapping?
   What does this add to the story?

10. What is the effect on the story of the recurring idea of sons hating their fathers and wanting to kill them?
    Give reasons for your answer.

11. In every chapter, characters offer revealing, honest accounts of their lives and personal suffering.
    What does this style of storytelling add to the story?

12. Is this a simple or complex story?
    Explain your point of view.

13. Who would enjoy this story?
    Who is this story intended for?
    Give reasons for your answer.

14. What makes us invest ourselves emotionally in the lives of characters in this novel?

15. Do you feel you know these characters well?
    How has the author achieved this effect?

16. Is Bobby's character likeable?
    Give reasons for your answer.
    Is Bobby's character relatable?

Give reasons for your answer.
How does Bobby's character add to the storytelling in this novel?

17. Is Bobby Mahon an effective lead character?
Did you become involved in his story?
Is he a typical hero?
Use examples to support your ideas.

18. What obstacles is Bobby met with during the novel?
How well does he deal with these difficulties?
Include examples in your answer.

19. Is Bobby described in very positive terms throughout the story?
How does this affect the narrative and the reading experience?
Use examples to illustrate your ideas.

20. Are you disappointed that there was not a second chapter from Bobby's perspective at the end of the story?
Explain your point of view.

21. Would you go on holidays with Bobby? Why/why not?

22. Would you trust Bobby with your car/phone/house keys? Why/why not?

23. How are mental health problems presented in the text?
Is this a success or flaw in the narrative?
Give reasons for your answer.

24. Is there humour in this novel?
    How does it add to the story?

25. Comment on the story's pacing.
    Does it add to reader enjoyment, in your view?

26. How does the author create depth and complexity in his characters?
    Be specific in your answer.

27. Are their some similarities between the 'bad' characters in the story?
    What does this add to the novel?

28. How does imagining the characters as you read add to the storytelling?

29. Is this a very visual text?
    How does this impact on your enjoyment of the story?

30. Comment on the mood as the story ends.

31. How does setting contribute to the story?

32. Do you find this novel to be interesting and easy to follow?
    What draws the audience into this story?
    Highlight specific aspects of the the text in your answer.

33. Where do you see conflict in this story?
    How does the use of conflict add to this story?

34. Is this a realistic story?
    Support your view.

35. Is this story predictable?
    Did you expect Bobby to have killed his father?
    Did you expect Bobby to assert his innocence?
    How does the author make you question your view of Bobby?
    Did you expect the kidnapped boy to be found alive?
    Was this a satisfactory conclusion to this strand of the narrative?
    How does Dylan's safe recovery impact on the story's ending?

36. Did you enjoy this story?
    Use examples from the text to support your answer.

37. Who is your favourite character in this novel?
    What makes you like/admire them?

38. Who is your least favourite character in this novel?
    What makes you dislike them?

39. What themes can you identify in this story?

40. Is this novel about loss?
    Explain your view.

41. One reviewer said, "a great strength of the book is Ryan's ability to capture the vernacular of contemporary Ireland". What does the author's use of vernacular speech bring to the story?

Did you enjoy this aspect of the novel?
Give reasons for your answer.

42. Is 'The Spinning Heart' an emotionally engaging text?
Does it offer emotional depth and complexity?
Explain your point of view.

43. How does the layering technique, with chapters overlapping, add tension and suspense?

44. Is Bobby's chapter the most significant chapter in the novel?
How does this impact on the novel as a whole?

45. Do you get a good sense of the speakers in each chapter and the type of people they are?
How does the author achieve this?

46. What does Frank's ghost add to the narrative?
Is this supernatural aspect significant, in your view?

47. Has Bobby's name been cleared by the end of the story?
Is this significant?
Does this impact on your enjoyment of, and satisfaction in, the ending?

48. Is Jim Gildea a hero as the story ends?
Why/why not?

49. How does Dylan being found alive impact on the story's ending?

50. Are significant voices absent in the novel?
    Is there anybody else you would have liked to have heard from?

51. Do you like the novel's ending?
    Is it a happy ending?
    Is it satisfying from a reader's perspective?
    Explain your point of view.

# General Vision and Viewpoint

*General Vision and Viewpoint refers to the author's outlook or view of life and how this viewpoint is represented in the text.*

The overwhelming feeling in this novel is one of sadness, loss and regret, making the outlook very bleak and troubled. The story focuses on the hurt and sorrow caused by damaged, failed relationships, the private anguish of characters and the violence and judgement of their world, making the general vision and viewpoint very dark indeed.

Bobby Mahon hates his father who has treated him with contempt his whole life, to the point that Bobby imagines himself killing the older man. This dark idea of patricide is echoed by other speakers, including Bobby's father, and is fulfilled by Denis, who imagines he kills his own father as he beats Frank, ending his life. The rage fuelled violence of Denis' crime, and the hatred these men feel for their fathers, offers a hopeless view of life, where relationships that should be warm and supportive are destructive and abusive, and leave characters carrying a burden of rage and resentment for years.

Similarly, Lily's account of being beaten by her unborn child's father is shocking and saddening. Bernie punches her in the stomach when he learns she is carrying his child. He visits her only once more, to punch her in the face for naming him as the child's father when she was in hospital. The violence and hatred here, coupled with Bernie's indifference towards his child, adds to the dark view of life offered in the text.

There are many dark and sad moments in the story including Bridie's account of her son's drowning, Vasya's account of his brother's death, Timmy's sad upbringing and the breakdown of Bobby's relationship with his mother. These examples all add to the pervading sense of loss and sadness in the novel. Characters' accounts are full of failed dreams and dashed hopes, they seem trapped within their unhappy lives, struggling with despair and sorrow.

The novel is marked by a powerful sense of regret and what might have been. Characters lament the financial crisis, their personal situations, and how their lives have turned out. Both Vasya and Bridie lead isolated lonely lives, victims of tragedy they could not recover from.

The author creates a view of life that is difficult and trying, full of sadness and despair, where characters suffer alone. Destructive relationships compound these problems, filling characters with anger and hurt.

Another negative aspect that affects the general vision and viewpoint is that in 'The Spinning Heart' it is not enough to be yourself, for characters are unhappy with who they are, longing to be someone else in order to escape their problems, inadequacies and shortcomings. Seanie Shaper suffers alone with his depression, wishing he could be how everyone thinks he is. Brian wishes he could be Bobby, and calls himself a loser. Life is hard for these characters and they feel very negatively about themselves, which darkens the outlook and adds sadness to it. Despite their insight into their unhappiness, characters' paths seem fixed, with few hoping for change. This acceptance of life's failings, disappointments and sorrows adds to the bleak outlook of the text.

This dark outlook, although very powerful, is not completely relentless. Hope appears in the form of Bobby's loving relationship with his wife, and the devotion they feel towards one another. Bobby says he is not good enough for Triona, recognising her worth and showing gratitude for her. Similarly, she is devoted to Bobby, never believing that he was unfaithful, and saying that she would not care if Bobby had killed his father. For Triona, not even an act of murder would shake her belief in her husband or change how she feels about him, a very committed outlook indeed.

A second aspect that brightens the outlook at the novel's end is Dylan's safe recovery. With Jim Gildea's rescue comes hope and redemption, a tragedy has been averted, showing the possibility that life can be good, optimistic and joyful.

Therefore, overall, the general vision and viewpoint suggests a grim, trying view of life, full of human sadness and suffering, with a glimmer of hope and happiness in its ending. The lasting impression on the reader is one of having been through a very harrowing and difficult time, with the possibility of better things to follow.

1. Is there a sense of sadness in this novel?
   Use examples to support your ideas.

2. Is there a sense of loss in the novel?
   Use examples to support your view.
   How does this affect the general vision and viewpoint?

3. Is life fair for characters in this novel?
   Are they victims of bad luck and poor treatment?
   Is this an accurate view of life?
   Explain your point of view.

4. Does this novel suggest that everyone has a secret self?
   What sort of people are these secret selves?
   What does this suggest about life?
   How does this make you feel?

5. Are there many types of personal unhappiness in this story?
   What does this suggest about life?

6. How do characters feel about the economy and the state of the country?

7. Are there employment opportunities for characters in the novel?
   How does this impact on their happiness?
   How does this impact on the atmosphere and mood of the story?
   Do characters feel good about their lives?
   Use examples to support your view.

8. In this novel, is doing your best good enough?
   Is this a comforting or upsetting thought?

9. How do characters feel about themselves and their lives?
   How does this influence the general vision and viewpoint?

10. How do you feel when you read that Bobby has allegedly killed his father?

11. Is reading this novel a bleak or harrowing experience?
    Explain your point of view.

12. Is this a story of relentless sorrow? Or, are characters merely expressing to the reader what they cannot say to anyone else?
    How does this affect the outlook?

13. Do characters in 'The Spinning Heart' experience love in their lives?
    What does this suggest about life?

14. Is happiness possible for these characters?
    Is their outlook hopeful?

15. Is there hope in this story?
    Will life improve for these characters?
    Why/why not?
    Explain your point of view.

16. Does Bobby emerge as a kind, positive character?
    Is he the only positive character in the novel?
    What does this suggest about life?

17. Are there many negative characters in the novel?
    Why do they behave and feel as they do?
    What does this suggest about life?
    Does it show the positive or negative side of human nature?

18. By showing us such sorrow and private suffering, is the author trying to teach us something?
    Is there a positive message here?

19. How does your view of Bobby impact on the general vision and viewpoint?

20. Do regret or loneliness affect the general vision and viewpoint of the novel?
    Give reasons for your answer.

21. What does Bobby's relationship with Triona suggest about love?
    How does this impact on the novel's outlook?
    Give reasons for your answer.
    How does this affect the view of life offered in the novel?

22. What does Bobby's relationship with his father suggest about love?
    How does this impact on the novel's outlook?
    Give reasons for your answer.
    How does this affect the view of life offered in the novel?

23. Do characters in this novel have opportunities and the potential for happiness?
    How does this add to the novel's outlook?
    What does it suggest about life?

24. As the novel ends, do you feel optimistic about Bobby and Triona's future?
    Give a reason for your answer.
    Are you happy with how things have turned out?

25. Do characters generally have an optimistic or pessimistic approach to life?
    What does this suggest about life?

26. How do the murder and kidnapping storylines impact on the general vision and viewpoint?
    What do they suggest about people, and life?

27. Is love sure to succeed in this world?
    Explain your point of view.

28. Are characters in this text hopeful and forward looking about life?
    What does this suggest about their outlook in life?

29. What does this novel suggest about human nature?
    Is this outlook positive or negative?

30. Does the novel end on a hopeful or hopeless note?

31. Is life to be enjoyed or endured in the world of this text?
    Refer to the text to support your ideas.

32. What is the message behind this novel?
    What is the author, Donal Ryan, telling us about life in this story?
    Is this an encouraging, uplifting or depressing outlook?
    Give reasons for your answer.

# Theme/Issue
# Relationships

*Relationships has been selected as the theme/issue to explore in relation to this text.*

*The theme of relationships can be applied to any relationship in a text and includes love, marriage, friendship and family bonds. Consider the complexities of relationships and the impact they have on characters' lives.*

The negative relationships in 'The Spinning Heart' are one of the most compelling aspects of the story, and are a very significant theme in the novel. Bobby Mahon's relationship with his father is extremely flawed and lacks any sort of warmth or positive feeling. He hates his father for the cruel and vicious way his father has always treated him and his mother, destroying their bond with his watchfulness and sharp words.

Negative relationships are not just seen with Bobby and Frank, but with Frank and his own father, with Mags and her father, with Denis and his father and with Lily and Bernie, to mention but a few examples. Negative relationships are common, cropping up repeatedly throughout the story, often with unhappy consequences. Frank Mahon is viciously beaten by his father, and goes on to be a cruel, snide father and husband, perpetuating negative, hurtful behaviour, adding to the cycle of hurt and anger.

In this novel, negative relationships are characterised with violence, aggression, and a lack of warm feeling, support or kindness. Fathers in particular are seen to be distant, uncommunicative and unable to act lovingly, with many using violence to communicate how they feel. This is a very negative portrayal of relationships. The consequences of these damaged and damaging relationships are clearly seen in the suffering of characters in their heartfelt accounts. Denis, for example, commits murder, thinking he is killing his own father, such is his hatred of the man.

We see the positive side of relationships in Bobby's relationship with his wife Triona. He is a devoted husband, who loves and values his wife, while she too is steadfast in her love of, and belief in, him. Their love and commitment is a positive comment on the theme of relationships. However, their relationship is not perfect, marred by Bobby's inability to open up to Triona and talk to her. Overall though, considering the extent of hateful and hurtful relationships in the text, Bobby and Triona's marriage is a complete contrast, suggesting a very loving and loyal, though not perfect, relationship.

1. What strikes you about Bobby's relationship with his father?
   Is this a positive or negative relationship?
   Give reasons for your answer.

2. Does Bobby's relationship with his father bring him sorrow or joy?
   Explain your point of view.

3. Describe Bobby's relationship with his father.
   How does Bobby feel about Frank?
   How does he treat his father?
   How does Frank feel about Bobby?
   How does he treat his son?

4. Is Bobby's relationship with his father very damaged and destructive, in your view?
   Give reasons for your answer.

5. Are there any positives in Bobby's relationship with his father?
Fully explain your point of view.

6. What sort of relationship did Bobby have with his mother?
What damaged his relationship with his mother?
How does this add to the theme of relationships?

7. How have Bobby's damaged relationships with his parents impacted on him as a person?
Give reasons for your answer.

8. What strikes you about Bobby's relationship with Triona?
Is this a positive or negative relationship?
Give reasons for your answer.

9. Does Bobby's relationship with his wife bring him sorrow or joy?
Explain your point of view.

10. What strengths do you see in Bobby and Triona's relationship?

11. What weaknesses or problems do you see in Bobby and Triona's relationship?

12. What complicates Bobby and Triona's relationship?

13. Are Bobby and Triona a good match?
Explain your view.

14. Is Bobby devoted to Triona?
    Is this a positive portrayal of relationships?
    Explain your view.

15. Is Bobby's relationship with his father, or his relationship with Triona, the most significant relationship in the novel?
    Use examples to support your point of view.

16. Is the idea of sons hating abusive fathers significant in the novel?
    What does this bring to the theme of relationships?

17. Are relationships in this text very complicated?
    Explain your point of view.

18. Are relationships in this text marked by violence?
    Explain your point of view.

19. What stops characters from saying exactly how they feel to loved ones?
    Use examples to support your ideas.

20. Overall, are relationships depicted positively or negatively in this text?
    Do relationships bring characters happiness or sorrow?
    Use examples to support your point of view.

# Hero, Heroine, Villain

*'Hero, Heroine, Villain' refers to studying central characters (protagonists/ antagonists).*

*Their traits, values, etc. and their ability to deal with conflict, challenges, obstacles, etc. should be considered.*

Bobby Mahon, the story's hero, emerges as a decent, sensitive character who is well respected and admired in his community.

His account is very open and honest, and he tells the reader about his awful relationship with his father, and the loss and sadness he feels over his mother's death. Bobby's openness and vulnerability makes him very likeable and relatable. It is easy to understand how he is feeling and empathise with him.

Despite the poor economic climate, Bobby has not given up, and continues to look for small jobs to earn an income. This suggests perseverance and a refusal to give up, which are very positive traits.

Bobby is suspected for his father's murder, which shakes our belief in his goodness. However, many characters comment on Frank Mahon's horrible ways, almost suggesting that it would be understandable to kill him, making this crime seem more acceptable. Denis' account however clears Bobby's name for the reader, and affirms that he has not done such a thing. Similarly, there are rumours that Bobby has had an affair, which turn out to be nothing more than gossip. In both cases, these accusations make us question what we know of Bobby, but his innocence shows he is a good, loyal man. In fact, these untrue rumours and gossip may make the reader feel sorry for him and relate to him more.

Bobby is seen as a natural leader. Rory's parents view him as somebody that gets things done, and Brian wishes he was Bobby. This admiration adds to the sense of Bobby as a very positive character, as do the references to him being handsome and a good athlete. Overall, Bobby is described as someone very loyal, hardworking and decent, with hidden depths and a sensitive side to his character.

1. What are your impressions of Bobby from the opening chapter?

2. Does your view of Bobby change during the story? Give reasons for your answer.

3. How does Bobby feel about his father?
How does Bobby treat his father?
What does this tell you about his character?

4. How does Bobby feel about his wife?
How does Bobby treat his wife?
What does this tell you about his character?

5. Is Bobby a likeable character?
Give reasons for your answer.
Is Bobby a relatable character?
Give reasons for your answer.

6. Many characters in the text admire and look up to Bobby. Why is this the case?

7. Bobby is often described as being sound.
What does this mean?
Why do other characters describe him this way?
Use examples to support your view.

8. Is Bobby described in very positive terms?
   Use examples to support your view.

9. What sort of life has Bobby had?
   How has this affected him as a person?

10. Is Bobby faced with a lot of challenges and problems in the novel?
    How does he deal with these challenges and problems?
    What is your response to this?

11. Did you suspect Bobby of killing his father?
    Give reasons for your answer.

12. Did you suspect Bobby of having an affair?
    Give reasons for your answer.

13. Do you like Bobby Mahon?
    What makes you feel this way about him?

14. Is Bobby a typical hero? Explain your point of view.

15. Is Bobby a damaged character?
    Explain your point of view, using examples to support your ideas.

16. Is Bobby a vulnerable character?
    Is this an appealing feature?
    Explain your point of view.

17. Would you trust Bobby with your car/phone/house keys?
    Why/why not?

18. Would you go on holidays with Bobby?
    Why/why not?

19. If you could offer Bobby some advice, what would it be?
    Give a reason for your answer.

# Selecting Key Moments

The following is a list of key moments from the novel.
For each moment, select which mode(s) it belongs to.
Write a short piece outlining what this moment tells you about this mode/adds to this mode in the novel.

- The opening, where Bobby Mahon and his life are introduced.
- Lily's description of Bernie's reaction when he learned he was her child's father.
- Brian's situation as he prepares to emigrate.
- The drowning of Bridie's son.
- Trevor's plan to kidnap Dylan and sweep Réaltín off her feet.
- Learning of Frank Mahon's murder.
- Learning of the kidnapping of Dylan.
- Seanie Shaper's depression.
- The kidnapper's perspective.
- Denis admits to murder.
- Frank's reflections on his life.

- Triona's description of how she feels about Bobby.
- The news that Dylan is safe and well.

# The Comparative Study: Comparing Texts

*Use the following questions to compare your texts, noting the similarities and differences between them. Include examples to support the points that you make.*

## Cultural Context/Social Setting

*Consider each of your chosen texts in your answers.*

1. In which of the texts you have studied for the Comparative Study do characters have the most freedom and choice?
   Why is this the case?
   Justify your answer with examples from your chosen texts.

2. In which of your texts are characters most controlled?

3. Who holds the power in each world?
   Who is powerless?

4. In which world is difference most accepted and respected?
   In which world is difference least accepted and respected?

5. Which world is the least tolerant?
   Which world is the most tolerant?
   Include examples to explain your view.

6. Which world is the best to live in if you are a woman? Give reasons for your answer.

7. Which world is the best to live in if you are a man? Give reasons for your answer.

8. Which world is the best to live in if you are a child? Give reasons for your answer.

9. Which text portrays the most violent and volatile world?

10. Which of your texts portrays the safest, most secure place?

11. Which of your texts portrays the most supportive world?

12. Which of these worlds is the darkest, most fearful place?

13. Which of these worlds is the brightest, most joyful place?

14. Which of these places is the most unpredictable?

15. Which text portrays the most traditional world?

16. Which of these societies holds family in the highest esteem?

17. Which of these societies holds love in the highest esteem? Which of these societies holds love in the lowest esteem?

18. Which of these societies holds religion in the highest esteem?

Which of these societies holds religion in the lowest esteem?

19. Which of these societies holds power in the highest esteem?

20. Which of these societies holds wealth in the highest esteem?

21. Where do you see the best treatment of the vulnerable of society? Include examples to support your view.

22. Where do you see the worst treatment of the vulnerable of society? Include examples to support your view.

23. Which of the worlds you have studied is the most materialistic?
Which of the worlds you have studied is the least materialistic?
What makes characters have these outlooks?

24. Which of the worlds you have studied is the most secretive?
What makes characters behave this way?

25. Which of your texts displays the greediest world?
What makes characters have this attitude?

26. Where is love most important?
Where is love most successful?
Where is love least important?
Where is love least succesful?

Compare the success of love in each of your chosen texts. What does this tell you about the worlds of these texts and characters' lives?

27. Which of these worlds appealed to you most? Give reasons for your answer.

28. Which of these worlds appealed to you least? Explain your point of view.

29. Which of your texts is home to the most religious or spiritual world?

30. Which of your texts showed the least religious or spiritual society?

31. How important is social class in each of your texts?

32. In which of your texts are characters most accepting of their world and society?

33. In which of your texts do characters challenge their world, society and values most?

34. In which of your texts do you see the greatest inequality?

35. In which of your texts do you see the greatest injustice?

36. Where do characters behave the best towards one another?
How does Cultural Context/Social Setting influence their behaviour?

37. How do characters reflect the Cultural Context/Social Setting of their worlds?
Explain, including examples.

38. How does the Cultural Context/Social Setting of your texts lead to problems and difficulties for the texts' characters?
How does it affect characters' responses to these difficulties?

39. Which key moments best capture the Cultural Context/Social Setting of each of your texts?

40. What similarities do you notice in the Cultural Context/Social Setting of this text and your other Comparative Study texts?

41. What differences do you notice in the Cultural Context/Social Setting of this text and your other Comparative Study texts?

## Literary Genre

1. Did you like the way this story was told more than your other Comparative Study texts?
State what you enjoyed most (and least) about each.

2. Is this text more exciting than your other texts?
Consider tension, suspense, pacing, conflict and the author's use of the unexpected.

3. How does the author make use of tension in each of your chosen texts?
Where is it most effective?
Where is it least effective?
Use examples to support your point of view.

4. How does the author make use of climax in each of your chosen texts?
Where is it most effective?
Where is it least effective?
Use examples to support your point of view.

5. How does the author make use of resolution in each of your chosen texts?
Where is it most effective?
Where is it least effective?
Use examples to support your point of view.

6. Are characters more engaging in this text than in your other texts?
Refer to each of your texts in your answer.

7. How does the author create vivid, memorable characters in each of your chosen texts?

8. In which of your texts are characters most life-like and compelling?
In which text are characters least life-like and most difficult to relate to?
Refer to each of your texts in your answer.

9. Is the setting more effective in telling the story in this text, than in your other texts?

10. Is this text more unpredictable than your other texts?
Refer to each of your texts in your answer.

11. Does this text have greater emotional power than your other texts?
Was this emotional power created in a more interesting way here or in a different text?
Refer to each of your texts in your answer.

12. What was your favourite literary technique, used by the author of each of your texts?
How did the use of this technique help the storytelling?

13. To what extent are you influenced by the point of view that this story is told from?
Are you influenced to a greater or lesser degree by the point of view utilised in your other Comparative Study texts?

14. Which key moments best capture Literary Genre in each of your texts?

15. What similarities do you notice in the Literary Genre of this text and your other Comparative Study texts?
Mention specific aspects of narrative.

16. What differences do you notice in the Literary Genre of this text and your other Comparative Study texts?
Mention specific aspects of narrative.

# General Vision and Viewpoint

1. Is life happier and fuller for characters in this text than in your other Comparative Study texts?
   Explain your point of view fully.

2. Do characters in this text face more obstacles and difficulties than in your other texts?
   Who struggles most?

3. Are characters in this text rewarded more for their struggles than in your other texts?
   Do they overcome adversity and achieve true happiness and contentment in a way that is not realised in your other texts?

4. How do events in these texts, and your personal response to these events, help your understanding of the General Vision and Viewpoint of these texts?
   Include specific examples in your answer.

5. How does your attitude to central characters help shape your understanding of the General Vision and Viewpoint of your chosen texts?
   Include specific reference to your chosen characters in your answer.

6. What aspects of this text did you respond to emotionally?
   How does this help your understanding of the General

Vision and Viewpoint of the text?
How does this compare to your other texts?

7. Is this the brightest, most hopeful and triumphant text you have studied?
Explain why its message is more or less positive than in your other texts.

8. Which of your chosen texts was the bleakest and most upsetting or depressing?
Explain what made it more negative than your other texts. What made them more positive?

9. Plot your three texts on a scale of one to ten from darkest (most pessimistic) to brightest (most optimistic). Add a note to explain their positions.

10. Which key moments best capture the General Vision and Viewpoint of each of your texts?

11. What similarities do you notice in the General Vision and Viewpoint of this text and your other Comparative Study texts?

12. What differences do you notice in the General Vision and Viewpoint of this text and your other Comparative Study texts?

13. Can you relate any aspect of this text to your own life experience?
If so, how does this help to shape your understanding of the General Vision and Viewpoint of this text?

# Theme/Issue - Relationships

1. Are relationships in this text more positive and supportive than the relationships in your other chosen texts?
   Include specific examples in your answer.

2. Rank the relationships you have studied in your various texts from most positive (score of 10) to most negative (score of 1).
   Add a note explaining your choices.

3. Are relationships in this text the most engaging and interesting that you have studied?
   Explain your choice.

4. Rank the relationships you have studied in your various texts from the most interesting (score of 10) to the least interesting (score of 1).
   Add a note explaining your choices.

5. How do the events of the text impact on the characters' relationships with one another in this text and your other chosen texts?
   Who is most affected?
   Who is least affected?

6. How does conflict impact on the relationships of characters in this text and your other chosen texts?
   Who is most affected?
   Who is least affected?

7. How does social class impact on the relationships of characters in this text and your other chosen texts?
Who is most affected?
Who is least affected?

8. Is the theme of relationships portrayed in an idealistic or realistic way in each of your chosen texts?

9. Did any aspect of the theme of relationships shock or surprise you in your three chosen texts?
Use examples from your texts to support the points that you make.

10. What are the most interesting aspects of the theme of relationships in each of your chosen texts?

11. Which text taught you most about relationships?
Refer to each text in your answer.

12. Which key moments best capture the theme of relationships in each of your texts?

13. What similarities do you notice in the theme of relationships in this text and your other Comparative Study texts?

14. What differences do you notice in the theme of relationships in this text and your other Comparative Study texts?

# Hero/Heroine/Villain

*Consider the following list of questions for a central character in each of your chosen texts.*

1. Who is the most interesting character in the text?
   What makes them interesting?
   What do you like about them?
   What do you dislike about them?
   What are this character's strengths?
   What are this character's weaknesses?

2. How does this character cope with conflict?

3. How does this character cope with the unexpected?

4. Are they a resourceful character?

5. Are they an emotional character?
   Use examples to support your view.

6. Do you empathise with this character? Why/why not?

7. What do you admire about this character?

8. How well does this character relate to and interact with other characters?
   Include examples to support your points.

9. Is this character happy or sad?

10. Are they an active or passive character?
    How do they contribute to the action and storyline of the text?
    Are they important to the story's plot and development?

11. Is this character a good (successful and interesting) main character?

12. Would you like to meet this character?
    If you met them, what would you talk about?

13. If you had any advice for this character, what would it be?

14. Does this character make the story more exciting?
    In what way do they do this?

15. Is this character a hero/heroine or a villain?
    Explain your choice.

16. Identify the key moments in the text that illustrate your chosen character's personality traits/character.

17. On a scale of one to ten (with one being extremely heroic and ten being an evil villain), where would you place your chosen character?
    Give reasons for your choice.
    Where would you place the main characters from your other texts?
    Why would you place them here?

18. Which of your chosen characters do you like and admire most?

What makes them your favourite character?
Give reasons for your answer.

19. Which of your chosen characters do you dislike most?
Explain why you like some more than others.

20. Which of your chosen characters shocked you most?
Give reasons for your answer.

21. Which of your chosen characters impressed you most?
Give reasons for your answer.

22. Which of your chosen characters did you feel most sorry for?
Give reasons for your answer.

23. Who is the most resourceful character you have come across?
Give reasons for your answer.

24. Which of your chosen characters faced the most problems and difficulties?
Did they cope well with these problems?

25. How is your favourite character similar to the characters in your other texts?

26. How is your favourite character different to the characters in your other texts?

27. Choose key moments from each of your texts to highlight your characters' strengths and weaknesses.

www.ingramcontent.com/pod-product-compliance
Lightning Source LLC
Chambersburg PA
CBHW071449080526
44587CB00014B/2043